The Motif of the Journey in Nineteenth-Century Italian Literature

THE MOTIF OF THE
Journey
IN NINETEENTH-CENTURY ITALIAN LITERATURE

*Edited by Bruno Magliocchetti
and Anthony Verna*

Introduction by M. H. Abrams

UNIVERSITY PRESS OF FLORIDA

*Gainesville/Tallahassee/Tampa/Boca Raton
Pensacola/Orlando/Miami/Jacksonville*

Copyright 1994 by the Board of Regents of the State of Florida
Printed in the United States of America on acid-free paper ∞
All rights reserved

99 98 97 96 95 94 6 5 4 3 2 1

A modified version of Gustavo Costa's chapter, "Ugo Foscolo's Europe: A Journey from the Sublime to Romantic Humor," was published in *Symposium* 47, no. 2 (Summer 1993): 98–111. The chapter is published here in its original form as read for the symposium "The Motif of the Journey in Nineteenth-Centry Italian Literature." The portions that appeared in *Symposium* are reprinted by permission of the Helen Dwight Reid Educational Foundation. Published by Heldref Publication, 1319 18th Street, Washington, D.C. 20036-1802. Copyright 1993.

Library of Congress Cataloging-in-Publication Data

The Motif of the journey in nineteenth-century Italian literature / edited by Bruno Magliocchetti and Anthony Verna; introduction by M. H. Abrams.
p. cm.
Papers presented at a symposium held at the University of Toronto in the spring of 1989.
Includes bibliographical references and indexes.
ISBN 0-8130-1291-0
1. Travel in literature—Congresses. 2. Italy in literature—Congresses. 3. Italian literature—19th century—Themes, motives—Congresses.   I. Magliocchetti, Bruno. II. Verna, Anthony.
PQ4053.T75M68   1994
850.9'355—dc20   94-8388

The University Press of Florida is the scholarly publishing agency for the State University System of Florida, comprised of Florida A & M University, Florida Atlantic University, Florida International University, Florida State University, University of Central Florida, University of Florida, University of North Florida, University of South Florida, and University of West Florida.

University Press of Florida
15 Northwest 15th Street
Gainesville, FL 32611

Preface / vii

INTRODUCTION
Spiritual Travelers in Western Literature
M. H. Abrams / 1

CHAPTER ONE
Ugo Foscolo's Europe:
A Journey from the Sublime to Romantic Humor
Gustavo Costa / 21

CHAPTER TWO
The Italian Journey: From James to Eliot to Browning
Eleanor Cook / 41

CHAPTER THREE
Giacomo Leopardi: Journey from Illusions to Truth
G. Singh / 53

CHAPTER FOUR
Of Swallows and Farewells: The Morality of Movement
in Italian Literature of the *Ottocento*
Antonino Musumeci / 70

CHAPTER FIVE
Italie-Italies: Typo/Topologies of French Travel Accounts
in the Nineteenth Century
Christian Bec / 84

CHAPTER SIX
The Significance of the Journey in Manzoni
S. B. Chandler / 94

CHAPTER SEVEN
Verga, or The Impossible Journey
Romano Luperini / 107

CHAPTER EIGHT
The Journey in Ippolito Nievo's Narrative: Typologies
Marinella Colummi Camerino / 126

CHAPTER NINE
Travel as Inspiration in Pascoli's Poetry
V. R. Giustiniani / 141

CHAPTER TEN
New and Traditional Forms
of Nineteenth-Century Travel Literature
Elvio Guagnini / 150

Notes / 167

Contributors / 194

Index / 195

Preface

The essays collected in this volume are intended to explore one of the most enduring and central topoi in the literature of Western civilization. The richness and depth with which the motif of the journey has been invested in the literary production of all ages have made it necessary to limit our attention not only to the works of a single country but also to the authors of a single century.

If we accept the widely held view that the Romantic period constitutes a watershed in the history of modern European letters, then it would not be inconsistent to argue that the greatest corroboration of this position is the manner in which the motif of the journey is utilized by nineteenth-century authors. Although the authors who preceded the Romantic period—from Homer to St. Augustine, from Dante to Shakespeare, from Rousseau to Alfieri—all relied in fundamental ways on the theme of the journey to give form and structure to their spiritual and imaginative universe, those who followed radically expanded not just the creative potential of this time-honored metaphor but the very core of its moral and artistic significance.

Against this backdrop, M. H. Abrams's essay is instrumental in providing the critical and philosophical paradigms required to guide the reader through the textual journey resulting from the volume. Tracing the most vital and significant aspects of the master trope, as he calls the journey, from its biblical origins up to the twentieth century, the author argues that, despite the recurrence of many traditional elements in the application of this literary device, modern and contemporary epochs have added new and revolutionary horizons of meaning.

A metaphor with such a long and complex literary history, however, would be difficult, if not impossible, to appreciate fully without taking into account some of its own unique inconsistencies or contradictions. As we examine more closely the literary production of major nineteenth-century Italian authors, it will become clear that their interpretations of the journey are not infrequently at variance with the ones utilized by non-Italian writers of the period. To illustrate Italy's contribution to the history of the trope, at a time when countries became increasingly more interdependent and conscious of each other's cultures, is the principal goal that the present collection of essays strives to accomplish.

In his essay "Ugo Foscolo's Europe: A Journey from the Sublime to Romantic Humor," Gustavo Costa sensitively reconstructs not only the physical movement that takes Foscolo across many cultural and linguistic milieus, but also the literary itinerary that reflects the dynamics of his intellectual and artistic growth. From *Le ultime lettere di Iacopo Ortis* to the last and unfinished *Le Grazie* are the sources of further insights about an author whose similar journeys frequently intersect to arrive at different levels of signification and artistic achievement. By placing Foscolo between two well-defined and contrasting critical concepts—the sublime and Romantic humor—Costa paves the way for a clearer understanding of the poet's spiritual and artistic quests.

In "The Italian Journey: From James to Eliot to Browning," Eleanor Cook aptly illustrates the significance of Italy as a locus in the works of three English-speaking authors. The Italian journey that Cook highlights is a journey traced backward: a metalepsis. Specifically, she examines the reading journey that writers themselves take back through earlier writers, such as the one undertaken by James back through Eliot to Browning. This suggestive approach to the understanding of the *Bildungsreise* [educational journey] becomes especially rewarding in the works she analyzes. As an additional point, the author provides an appropriate sampling showing the potential for a feminist reading of the motif of the journey.

If Italy provided foreign authors with a privileged locus for their physical and spiritual journeys, it also gave European literature a most enduring lyrical voice. G. Singh's essay "Giacomo

Leopardi: Journey from Illusions to Truth," encapsulates in a cogent fashion the central concerns that lie behind the poet's artistic and philosophical discourse. The critic's compelling interpretation of Leopardi's incessant search for and acceptance of man's position in the universe is posited in terms of a philosophical journey that never deviates from the truth, no matter how unpalatable or transgressive that truth might be. The comparative thrust of Singh's timely and considered reappraisal of the poet's preeminent voice in European letters lends credibility to those who share the view that Leopardi has been unduly neglected.

Antonino Musumeci's "Of Swallows and Farewells: The Morality of Movement in Italian Literature of the *Ottocento*" offers the reader one of the most lucid expressions of the manner in which the negative attributes attached to the metaphor of the journey become the collective experience of an entire nation. In other words, boundaries are not just physical entities but are above all moral coordinates that provide the ground for social and individual values. The centrifugal forces of the journey, as the author eloquently demonstrates, become powerful imaginative constructs that lead to an espousal of rootedness and enclosure.

In a well-documented essay, Christian Bec outlines the rich catalogue of the numerous faces of Italy captured by French authors who crossed the Alps during the nineteenth century. The typo/topologies which emerged from their travel accounts reflect a widespread mannerism at the same time predictable and self-serving. Thus, the French writers who traveled to the Italian peninsula not only reinforced the common stereotypes and myths of Italian life but also contributed—paradoxically—to the fascination Italy and its people continued to hold for transalpine audiences. To elucidate the nature of such contacts, Bec makes a worthy contribution with his essay, "Italie-Italies: Typo/Topologies of French Travel Accounts in the Nineteenth Century."

"The Significance of the Journey in Manzoni" reflects S. B.

Chandler's long-standing interest in Italy's most important Romantic writer. The metaphor of life as a spiritual quest is reconstructed in a manner that shows Chandler's detailed knowledge of the author's works. On the basis of Manzoni's eschatological premises, Chandler is able to synthesize effectively the meaning of the trope as an emanation of a providential design.

Romano Luperini's essay, "Verga, or the Impossible Journey," is a fundamental contribution to the understanding of the author's narrative labyrinth. In his analysis, Luperini is able to demonstrate how the journey in Verga remains essentially disruptive, nonreintegrating, and nonredemptive. Entrance into the world of modernity, in both the historical and literary realms, is destined to bring about those conditions of human existence devoid of meaning and value. In this context, Luperini's insightful conclusion shows why, in Verga, the journey ultimately metamorphoses into mere vagabondage.

The composite nature of the trope of the journey in the works of Ippolito Nievo is the subject of Marinella Colummi Camerino's contribution to the volume. In her essay "The Journey in Ippolito Nievo's Narrative: Typologies," Colummi Camerino illustrates, in cogent and convincing terms, the dynamism of the metaphor as a vehicle through which we can glean the conflicting values of the urban and rural worlds, between bourgeois and peasant societies. At a broader and deeper level, life as a journey—as we see it through the eyes of the protagonist—suggests not only its fragmentary nature but, more important, its own precariousness.

Travel as a negative experience constitutes the core of V. R. Giustiniani's analysis of Pascoli's poetry. The poet's reluctance to appreciate the benefits of movement explains the critical stance with which Pascoli articulates the motif of the journey in his poetry. Giustiniani's essay, "Travel as Inspiration in Pascoli's Poetry," also delves into the poet's reinterpretations of the classical uses of the trope.

The concluding essay is provided by Elvio Guagnini. His "New and Traditional Forms of Nineteenth-Century Travel Literature" focuses on the growing importance of travel literature as a phenomenon in nineteenth-century Italian life and letters. As a catalyst for change, travel becomes according to the author an indispensable experience through which Italians are able to acquire greater cultural and scientific knowledge of themselves and of the rest of the world. The journeys Guagnini traces cross many geographical and disciplinary boundaries. He thus affords the reader a better understanding of travel literature and the way it impacted upon different genres as well as a variety of political and social domains.

As a final note, we wish to express our gratitude to all the participants in the symposium who, in many cases, undertook their own voyages from different countries to gather at the University of Toronto in the spring of 1989 to share with colleagues the results of their ongoing research on this subject. Special thanks are due to Professor M. H. Abrams who not only supported and encouraged this project from its inception but also agreed to provide a substantive introduction, which no one could have done in a more masterful manner. We wish to acknowledge our indebtedness to the following institutions and agencies whose generous financial and material support made the symposium possible: Department of Italian Studies, University of Toronto; Dean's Office, Faculty of Arts and Science, University of Toronto; Social Sciences and Humanities Research Council of Canada, Ottawa; Woodsworth College, University of Toronto; St. Michael's College, University of Toronto; Trinity College, University of Toronto; Victoria College, University of Toronto; Italian Cultural Institute, Toronto; and Alitalia, Toronto.

Introduction

SPIRITUAL TRAVELERS
IN WESTERN LITERATURE

M. H. Abrams

The essays collected in this book deal with some of the representations, in a single country and century, of one of the enduring master tropes by which the postclassical West has endowed the course of human life with structure, purpose, meaning, and values. This trope, the *peregrinatio vitae* [life's journeying], images the course of the life both of the human race and of the individual as an extended journey through alien lands. The major source of the image is found in the early books of the Hebrew Bible, with their narratives of diverse literal journeys that became archetypes for various figurative applications. Most prominent are the expulsion of Adam and Eve from Eden to sojourn in a fallen world; the punishment meted out to Cain, to wander as a fugitive and a vagabond in the earth; and the exile of Ishmael, son of Hagar, to live as "a wild man" whose hand will be against every man, and every man's hand against him.[1] The most sustained, detailed, and richly suggestive of the Old Testament journeys, however, is the exodus of the Hebrews "out of the land of Egypt, out of the house of bondage," their long wanderings in the wilderness in quest of the land promised to Abraham, Isaac, and Jacob; the journey of Moses up Mount Sinai to encounter Divinity; and his later ascent of Mount Pisgah for a glimpse of the Promised Land, to which access was denied him but was later granted his people.

The tendency to allegorize these and other stories of expulsions, punishments, escapes, quests, and migrations began in the later books of the Hebrew Bible itself and was given great impetus in the Christian Scriptures. Three scriptural passages—all of them probably written in the middle or later part of the first century—proved to be of great consequence for later forms and applications of the trope of the journey. In his Epistle addressed to the Hebrews (11:8–16), Paul represented the spiritual history of the Hebrew people hitherto in the vehicle of biblical narratives of exile, wandering, and pilgrimage in quest of a promised land—a promise that can now be fulfilled by the higher goal of a heavenly city. "By faith" Abraham and his descendants "sojourned in the land of promise as in a strange country," but died (as had Moses) "not having received the promises, but having seen them afar off . . . and confessed that they were strangers and pilgrims on the earth. For they that say such things declare plainly that they seek a country. . . . But now they desire a better country, that is, an heavenly: wherefore God . . . prepared for them a city."

The second and closely contemporary passage is Luke 15:11–32, which is explicitly identified as a parable, or short allegory, and is invested with the authority of Jesus himself. The passage represents the spiritual events of sin and repentance in human life in the narrative vehicle of the prodigal son who left home and father "and took his journey into a far country, and there wasted his substance with riotous living." Starving and penitent, he returned to his father, to be greeted with joy and feasting, "for this my son was dead, and is alive again; he was lost, and is found." In the process of time, this parable assimilated other Old Testament journey-narratives, was endlessly reiterated, and was often used to represent the totality of human history, from the fall and expulsion out of Eden to a coming redemption at the end of time. Of special historical consequence was the fact that the story of the prodigal son figured the spiritual history of humanity as, specifically, a circular journey that ends at the point of departure. Later commentators often interpreted the assertion of Jesus in John 14:6, "I am the way, the truth, and the life: no man cometh unto the Father but by me," as signifying a roundabout way—from home and father, into a far country, and back home.

The figure of human history as a circular return was abetted, and importantly supplemented, by a third passage, the vision of the end of earthly history that concludes both the Book of Revelation and the biblical canon. There the last things—to be accomplished by the God who is himself "the beginning and the end, the first and the last"—are described as a replication of the first things. The creation of heaven and earth "in the beginning" is to be matched by the advent of "a new heaven and new earth" at the end; the original felicity in Eden is to be restored, in that "there shall be no more death, neither sorrow nor crying," for "there shall be no more curse," while the locale of that felicity will include the "river of water of life" and "the tree of life" that had been essential features in the Garden of Eden. What had been a garden, however, is now replaced (as in the Epistle to the Romans) by a city; and this, in a portentous new development, is represented as not only a city but also a woman, "the holy city, new Jerusalem . . . prepared as a bride adorned for her husband." The consummation of history is accordingly imaged as a sacred marriage between the Lamb of God and this woman, his bride, while the compulsion to the human quest for consummation is described—in a way that was to resonate through later Western literature, whether sacred or profane—in the language of ardent desire: "And the Spirit and the bride say, Come. And let him that heareth say, Come. And let him that is athirst come."

Crucial to the development and widespread adoption of the Christian motif of the circular journey were the *Enneads* of the pagan philosopher Plotinus. Writing in the third century, Plotinus formulated a cosmic scheme in which everything emanates from the One (who is ipso facto the Good) through stages of increasing remoteness and division, to the ultimate stage of the material universe and the supervenience of evil. Counter to this eternal procession, however, is a ceaseless "epistrophe," or return to the origin; for "to Real Being we go back . . . to that we return as from that we came." (The Neoplatonist Proclus later formulated this radical metaphysical metaphor as "In any divine procession the end is assimilated to the beginning, main-

A. R. L. Ducros. *L'arco di Costantino* (Constantine's Arch). Musée Cantonal des Beaux-Arts, Lausanne, Switzerland.

taining by its reversion thither a circle without beginning without end."]² Repeatedly, Plotinus represents the longing of the soul to return to its origin in images that are consonant with those in the Christian Scriptures. The soul, for example, is pictured as a lover and the One as the beloved. Alternatively, the soul is described as an errant daughter who abandons her father for a mortal lover but later repents and once more seeks the father, and finds her peace. And in a reading of the Homeric epic that was to be echoed by many later writers, Plotinus interprets the circular voyage of Odysseus as an allegory for each person's internal journey in quest of the spiritual home and father that were earlier abandoned. Plotinus quotes the *Iliad* 2.140, "Let me flee to the beloved Fatherland": "This is the soundest counsel. But what is this flight? . . . For Odysseus is surely a parable to us when he commands the flight from the sorceries of Circe or Calypso. . . . The Fatherland to us is There whence we have come, and There is The Father."[3]

Wherever it came to be known, this worldscheme, with its rootmetaphor of emanation and return, exerted a profound attraction upon Christian theology, with the result that the personal God of the Bible, creator and redeemer of humankind, was to various degrees assimilated to the utterly abstract and impersonal first principle of Neoplatonic metaphysics. Conversely, however, the cosmic circulation of the Neoplatonic metaphysical system—timeless, unembodied, and as Proclus said, "without beginning and without end"—was by Christian exegetes temporalized, embodied in the process of human history, and figured as a single circle that at its end will return to its beginning, then stop.

By the close of the fifth century all these varieties of the spiritual journey, Christian and pagan, were deployed in the extraordinarily erudite and innovative writings of Saint Augustine. He adapted Plotinus's allegoric reading of Homer to the Christian pilgrimage: "Is the sentiment of Plotinus forgotten?— We must fly to our beloved fatherland. There is the Father, there our all. What fleet or flight shall convey us thither?"[4]

With this pagan figure of the circular voyage Augustine fused the narratives of exile, wandering, and quest for a promised land in the early books of the Bible, the figurative pilgrimage to "a better country" in the Epistle to the Hebrews, the circular journey of the prodigal son back to the home and father he has left, and the culminating vision in the Book of Revelation of the sacred marriage, supplemented by the candid expressions of erotic desire in the Song of Songs. The result was that Augustine established the full and enduring Christian topos of the *peregrinatio vitae*—the figure of fallen man, generic and individual, who wanders as an exile in an alien land, on a toilsome journey in quest of a city in another country that, when reached, turns out to be the home and father he left behind, and that often turns out also to be the dwelling of the bride he abandoned in the beginning. And, on the tacit assumption of early biblical hermeneutics that images signifying the same spiritual thing can be substituted for each other, Augustine often represented the conjoint origin and goal of the spiritual journey as a conflation of places, persons, genders, functions, and relationships that bewilders a reader untutored in the interchangeability of the signifiers in Christian typology:

> Let me enter into my chamber and sing my songs of love to Thee, groaning with inexpressible groaning in my pilgrimage, and remember Jerusalem with my heart stretching upwards in longing for it: Jerusalem my Fatherland, Jerusalem which is my mother: and remembering Thee its Ruler, its Light, its Father and Tutor and Spouse. . . . So that I shall not turn away but shall come to the peace of that Jerusalem, my dear mother. . . .
>
> For that City the friend of the bridegroom sighs . . . for he is a member of the Spouse of Christ; and he is jealous for it, for he is the friend of the bridegroom.[5]

Through the Middle Ages and beyond, spiritual renderings of biblical accounts of exiles and journeys, pilgrims and prodigals, served as commonplaces in numberless commentaries, sermons, homilies, and works of literature. In extended form, the *peregrinatio* constituted the total plot of that familiar allegoric narrative in which the protagonist is named Everyman, or Mankind, or Christian; in which the allegory signifies the normative course of a Christian life; and in which the goal of the traveler's laborious and dangerous quest is a land or city where one truly belongs, which frequently is the dwelling place of a woman of irresistible sexual attractiveness. The chivalric romances—with their literal plots of journeying knights, quests, and perilous trials by which the protagonist proves that he merits his lady love—obviously invited adaptation into allegories of the wayfaring Christian life. A late and elaborately designed instance is Spenser's *Faerie Queene.* The plot of the first book consists of the journey, quest, and trials of the faith and morality of the Red Cross Knight and ends with his betrothal to Una in the land of Eden, which he has just delivered from the dragon; this event prefigures the projected ending of the poem as a whole—the successful conclusion of Arthur's protracted search for the Faerie Queene, by whose beauty, seen in a vision, he had been ravished before the beginning of the narrative proper. Almost a century later, John Bunyan wrote the great working-class equivalent of the adventurous quest of the aristocratic knight on horseback, in his story of the pilgrim who shoulders his pack and trudges sturdily through commonplace obstacles, temptations, and perils, toward the celestial city for which he longs. Even in this demotic and puritan version, the motivation for the quest continues to be expressed in the language of sexual desire. When Christian and Hopeful finally arrive "within sight of the city they were going to," in the land where "the contract between the bride and the bridegroom was renewed," Christian "with desire fell sick," wherefore the travelers "lay by it a while, crying out because of their pangs, If you see my Beloved, tell him I am sick of love."[6]

The literature of the early nineteenth century, especially in Germany and England, was to a remarkable degree a literature of literal, allegorical, and symbolic travelers. One familiar type is the exiled and guilt-ridden wanderer—recognizably on the model of Cain and his later avatar the Wandering Jew—represented by Coleridge's penitent Ancient Mariner and Byron's impenitent Manfred. Another type, like the protagonist in Shelley's *Alastor*, wastes away in an insatiable quest for an inaccessible object, which is represented as a woman of irresistible allure. Most widespread, however, is the reemployment of the ancient trope of the *peregrinatio vitae*. The representation of the normative life as a toilsome but indefatigable journey toward an ultimate land or place constitutes the plot-form not only in the major literary kinds in verse and prose, but also in the many instances of *Universalgeschichte* (a summary of the cognitive and moral history of all humankind, from its origin to its future culmination) and in the genre of the partly fictionalized autobiography. And surprisingly, the same trope is deployed as both theme and organizing principle in the most prominent systems of German philosophy. In its distinctive Romantic version, however, the fifteen-hundred-year-old plot of the spiritual *peregrinatio* has undergone a drastic alteration: the goal of the journey has been transferred from heaven to earth and has been internalized and secularized. That is, the journey of life, which had hitherto been a sustained trial for admission to an otherworldly city, is now conceived as a process of self-education, self-discovery, and self-fulfillment in this world. In the economy of statement made possible by German compounds, the Christian *Heilsgeschichte* [salvation history] has modulated into the Romantic *Bildungsgeschichte* [history of education]; the goal that justifies the ordeal of human experience is located in experience itself and consists of the mature identity and function that the ordeal has served to form.

A landmark in the transformation of sacred history into a secular process of inner development is Lessing's *The Education of the Human Race*, published in 1780. Undertaking expressly to translate the "revealed truths" of the Bible into conceptual terms, the "truths of reason," Lessing converted the scriptural narrative of humankind's fall and coming redemption into the natural history of humankind's gradual education in reason and morality; interpreted the stages of civilization as advancing degrees of the maturation of the human race; and represented the educational process—both of the race and of the individual—in the persistent vehicle of a journey, compelled by an immanent teleology, along a *Weg* [path] or *Bahn* [road] toward a distant goal.

As a thinker of the Enlightenment, Lessing conceived the journey of humankind to be linear, in the mode of a progressive education toward the achievement of rational and moral perfection. The Romantic version of the *peregrinatio*, however, adopts the circular rather than the linear form of the ancient plot, but with a distinctive difference that fuses the concept of progress with that of a return to the origin. That is, the educational journey is not imaged simply as a two-dimensional circle but also as ascending along a third, or vertical dimension so as to form a spiral, so that the educational process is conceived as moving from an initial unity through multiple divisions back to a complex integrity which replicates the simple unity of the origin but on a higher level. In many versions of the Romantic spiral journey, the place of origin and return is also figured as the home the traveler left behind and toward which he is compelled back by a homesickness for the father, mother, and a lost sheltered place; but this place, once it has been recovered, proves to be of higher status than the original home because now it has been earned and as a result is for the first time properly recognized and adequately valued. In a number of instances the educational traveler is driven also by desire for a female figure, who turns out to be the beloved he heedlessly abandoned at the outset. In this latter mode of the Romantic *peregrinatio*, as in innumerable earlier examples, the father and home to which the prodigal returns has been fused with the bride of the Apocalypse, so that the motivation for the journey is erotic as well as nostalgic. The bride, however, now tends to be conceptualized into an abstract feminine principle, but one that is endowed with infinite allure. In the rendering with which Goethe concludes the second part of *Faust:*

> Das Ewig-Weibliche
> Zieht uns hinan.
>
> [The Eternal-Womanly
> Draws us above.]

This trope of the developing consciousness of the human race and individual as a circuitous journey—to reach, at the end, a superior level of its beginning—informs a great variety of literary works in the Romantic era. It is identifiable in Hölderlin's epistolary novel *Hyperion,* as well as in Novalis's visionary prose romance *Heinrich von Ofterdingen*—of which the leitmotif is "Wo gehen wir denn hin?" "Immer nach Hause" [Where are we going to then? Still homeward]—and serves also as a structural element in Novalis's verse "Hymnen an die Nacht."[7] In Blake's cosmic myth, the fall of humankind out of a primitive unity and its long recursion to a higher integrity is at times represented as the wanderings of a mental traveler seeking that "sweet golden clime" at the conclusion of his journey; and Blake pictures the consummation of human history as the sexual reconjunction of Albion with Jerusalem, the female contrary from which he was divided at the beginning. After its first act, in which Prometheus renounces divisive hate for integrative love, the plot of Shelley's *Prometheus Unbound* consists of the educational journey of Asia down through the underground realm of Demogorgon up, around, and back to her marital reunion with Prometheus. In his quasi-autobiographical prose fiction *Sartor Resartus,* Carlyle describes how Teufelsdroeckh, the foundling who is his protagonist, "lifts his *Pilgerstab* [Pilgrim staff] . . . and begins a perambulation and circumambulation of the terraqueous Globe." The quest of Teufelsdroeckh, that is, takes him on a great circle route around the world, during which he ever turns "full of longing . . . to that unknown Father" who might take him to his paternal bosom. This route turns out to be an educational journey through division and anguished isolation to his ultimate recognition that his seemingly alien earth—"now my heedy Mother, now my cruel Stepdame"— was in fact the home in which, educated by suffering, he may now live as a member of the family of humanity.[8]

Contemporary German philosophy incorporated the same radical metaphor—of a spiraling self-educational journey that leads back to its origin—but on a higher turning. The major subject-object metaphysical "systems" of that era are represented as ever on the move, compelled by the tension between internal polarities, antitheses, or dialectical "contradictions" toward the closure of the circle in an endstate that, since all intervening oppositions will be therein maintained but reconciled, constitutes a superior version of the undivided self-unity from which the process originated. And persistently, this progressive systemic movement is rendered in the figurative plot form of a *Bildungsreise* [educational journey], the restless journey of an exiled agent—named "ego," or "subject," or "consciousness," or "Spirit"—in quest of an ultimate reconciliation with its divided other or others, in a conclusion that is pictured as a return to the place from which it set out.

Fichte, for example, described *Wissenschaft* [science of knowledge], as beginning with the unity of the absolute ego, which posits the non-ego in itself and so inaugurates a sustained tension, which drives a process that concludes only when it reaches the point at which it "closes with its first principle, returns into itself, and accordingly becomes, by its own agency, completely closed."[9] He also represented universal human history in the pictured form of a circuitous *peregrinatio* of humankind from an inherited paradise of thoughtless self-unity toward a recovered paradise, which will be a superior one because it will have been earned by endeavors en route.

> The collective journey [*Weg*] which, according to this view, mankind pursues here below, is no other than a way back

to that point upon which it stood at the very beginning, and has no other goal but to return to its origin. [Driven out of the paradise of effortless and ignorant innocence, mankind] by effort and knowledge builds his paradise for himself according to the model of the one he has lost.[10]

Friedrich Schelling's *Transcendental Idealism* (1800) presents his version of the initial division of the subject into polarities that ultimately compel a circuitous return to the undivided origin. At one place Schelling describes this process by recuperating Plotinus's reading of the Homeric epic as signifying a circular spiritual voyage back to the home that has been left. Alienated nature, Schelling wrote, "is a poem" that, if unriddled, would disclose itself to be "the Odyssey of the spirit which, wonderfully deluded, in seeking itself, flees itself," and will reach its goal only when it "returns completely to itself," as a subject that recognizes it is itself the object it seeks.[11]

In his book of letters entitled *On the Aesthetic Education of Man*, Schiller recurrently images the history of civilization as a complex educational journey toward maturity through which "both the individual and the species as a whole must pass . . . if they are to complete the full circle of their destiny [*Kreis ihrer Bestimmung*]." His long essay *On Naive and Sentimental Poetry* develops this figure, representing the evolution of culture as a circuitous educational journey in which we (like the prodigal son) arrogantly storm "into an alien land," only to discover that "we desire with painful longing to go back home"—a home that is also identified as "a paradise, a state of innocence, a golden age." But this painful way out turns out in fact to be the way back, although to an infinitely higher form of the innocence and self-unity we have lost. "The road [*Weg*] upon which the modern poets are traveling is the same which mankind must travel, collectively and as individuals. Nature makes him in unity with himself; art divides and cuts him in two; through the ideal he returns to unity." In an important variant of the circuitous journey, however, that Schiller shares with Fichte,

Hölderlin, and others, he maintains that, since the goal of the journey is infinite while mankind's powers and possibilities are finite, "the ideal is an infinite which he can never reach," but can only approximate.[12] In this version of the motif we find the common Romantic view that "der Weg ist das Ziel" [the path is the goal], that the goal of the journey is the journey itself, as well as the distinctive Romantic ethos that the proper aim of humankind is an indomitable "Streben nach dem Unendlichen" [striving after the unending], in which the measure of dignity and greatness consists, not in absolute achievement, but in maintaining the discrepancy between infinite reach and finite grasp.

Wordsworth's *Prelude* of 1805 was a poetic autobiography, while Hegel's *Phenomenology of Spirit,* published two years later, was a historical propaedeutic to his philosophical system. The parallels between two such diverse undertakings provide a striking illustration of the way the *peregrinatio vitae* served as a radical metaphor both in works of Romantic literature and philosophy.

Wordsworth described his work as a "poem on my own poetical education," and his account of this education has persistent recourse to the image of a self-formative journey. The poem opens with a deliberate echo of the exodus from Egypt, as the poet departs on foot from the city that to him had been "a house / Of bondage"; in the course of this walk, which is at first desultory, he becomes "as a Pilgrim resolute" and sets out toward his goal, "the chosen Vale." In Wordsworth's retrospective narrative of his life, many of the crucial episodes are literal journeys on foot, which modulate into spiritual landscapes traversed by a metaphorical wayfarer. Wordsworth deploys the figure of the journey in a double application—on the one hand, to the educational course of his life "from stage to stage / Advancing" until it achieves the "consummation of the Poet's mind," and on the other, to his internal quest through his memories in the artistic process of composing the poem that narrates his life's journey. In symmetry with its first book, the last book of the *Prelude* opens with a literal walk; this time, however, he travels not on a level plain but up Mount Snowden where—in the tradition of definitive visions on a mountain established by Moses on Sinai—Wordsworth recognizes in the cloud-shrouded and moonlit landscape the outer correlation to his own poetic mind and imagination. The close of the poem rounds back to its narrative beginning as Wordsworth, confirmed in his mature identity and vocation as a poet, takes up his "permanent abode" in the Vale that, in the initial passage, he had chosen as the goal of his journey. And in the title of the opening book of *The Recluse*, to which his entire autobiography was designed as prelude, this goal of his life's pilgrimage, in accord with the ancient tradition of the circular journey, is identified as home—*Home at Grasmere*—and is at the same time conflated with Eden. But consonantly with the Romantic pattern of the spiral return, Wordsworth describes his achieved Eden as immensely superior to the original Eden because it has been earned in the painful course of this self-formative journey: "Here must be his Home, this Valley be his World."

> The boon is absolute; surpassing grace
> To me hath been vouchsafed; among the bowers
> Of blissful Eden this was neither given,
> Nor could be given—possession of the good
> Which had been sighed for, ancient thought fulfilled. . . .[13]

Hegel's metaphysical system is in ceaseless motion, and that motion, compelled by an internal, goal-directed tension of successive antitheses, is always circular. "The true," as he describes this timeless circulation in his preface to *The Phenomenology of Spirit*, "is its own becoming, the circle that presupposes its end as its goal and so has it for its beginning." But, he also says, the circling is always a spiraling upward, in that "this return to the beginning is also an advance." The *Phenomenology* narrates the history of the Spirit's painful process toward acquiring the knowledge of the systematic metaphysical truth [*Wissenschaft*]—a process that incorporates, within the temporal course of time and history, the timeless spiral pattern manifested in the truth toward which it unknowingly strives. The history of the Spirit, that is, evolves spirally from an original self-unity, through a passing over into its other, then into many successive others, toward the ultimate achievement of a higher reunion with itself. Hegel renders this history in the literary plot form of the self-educative journey of the Spirit, which is represented (in its aspect as the collective human consciousness) as though it were a single protagonist: "The task is to consider the general individual, the self-conscious Spirit, in its education [*Bildung*]," of which "the aim is the Spirit's insight into what it is that constitutes knowledge"—the knowledge that is articulated in Hegel's metaphysical system. Repeatedly this *Bildungsgeschichte*, both of the race and of each individual, is imaged in the traditional mode of the *Bildungsreise:* "To become genuine knowledge," the Spirit "has to work its way through a long journey [*Weg*]"; while "each individual consciousness must also pass through the contents of the educational stages of the general Spirit, but . . . as stages of a way [*Weg*] that has been prepared and leveled for him." This way can be considered as an educational pilgrimage and quest, "the way of the natural consciousness, which presses on to true knowledge."[14]

The denouement of Hegel's protracted quest narrative, which he calls the stage of absolute knowledge, is rendered in the form of a recognition scene, in which the Spirit, now fully "self-conscious," recognizes that the knowledge that has been its goal is in fact self-knowledge; the Spirit finally becomes aware of its own identity as constituting not less than everything and everyone, all of which had once been alienated from itself, but are now recollected, and so repossessed, by the act of ultimate awareness. This culmination of the self-educative way in a circuitous recursion to "the beginning from which we went out," although now "at a higher level," Hegel images in the time-honored figure of a spiritual return home, although it is a home where the Spirit has all along been without knowing it: at that moment at which the Spirit "has annulled and taken back into itself this alienation and objectification, it is at home with itself [bei sich ist] in its otherness as such."¹⁵ And since the homecoming that concludes the educational quest of the Spirit is achieved in Hegel's own consciousness, in his role as both a manifestation and an amanuensis of the Spirit, we in turn now recognize that Hegel's educational history of the Spirit has in fact been—like Wordsworth's *Prelude*—the autobiography of its own protagonist.

The Italian writers treated in this collection of essays thus possessed a rich and long-lived heritage of intellectual and imaginative treatments of the motif of the *peregrinatio*. Italian literature, of course, had itself produced the greatest of all literary instances of this central Christian plot form. Dante's spiritual history introduces in its opening line its root metaphor as the protagonist, "Nel mezzo del cammin di nostra vita" [midway in the journey of our life], is granted the vision of another journey, with a relay of guides, through hell and up through purgatory to the verge of the heaven of heavens—thence to return, if only temporarily, to his journey in this realm of the sun and the other stars. Furthermore, as several essayists note, Italy had itself been the goal of the standard Grand Tour, during the sixteenth and seventeenth centuries by scions of the aristocracy only, but in the eighteenth century also by the merely well-to-do; and this literal educational journey served as a model for the figurative educational journeys in Romantic literature and philosophy.

Although they have recognized antecedents and analogues, the literary journeys that are identified and described in the essays in this volume render the motif in distinctive ways that reflect the historical and cultural circumstances of nineteenth-century Italy, as well as the temperament and talent of the individual authors. Antonino Musumeci stresses the circumstance that in recent centuries Italy has been primarily a country of geographical boundaries to be guarded and respected rather than overpassed, with the result that a primary locus of values has been the circumscribed, secure place, the space of the family within the perimeter of the community. A consequence for nineteenth-century literature has been the absence of the aspect of the outward journey as a positive value, an adventurous or spirit-testing quest, and the prominence instead of its alternative aspect—rooted even deeper in the history of the topos—as an enforced exodus, or a perilous excursion into alien places that involves the severing of relationships and that exposes the protagonist to destructive forces.

Within such a paradigm, Marinella Colummi Camerino and Romano Luperini identify—in the novelists Nievo and Verga—the recurrent image of journeying between the village and the city, in which the village represents the archaic life of enduring seasonal rhythms and multiplex familial and communal bonds and the city represents the rootlessness, the isolation, and the aimless acquisitiveness and squanderings of the bourgeois economic world. These spiritual journeys recapitulate a familiar Romantic design of exile and of nostalgia for a return to the origin, but with a significant difference. Both Nievo and Verga, like a number of their Romantic predecessors in Germany and England, suggest that the goal of life's metaphorical journey, figured as the secure home that one has left behind, is inaccessible. But we do not find in these Italian writers the associated Romantic theme that the journey is itself the goal, and that success in life is measured by the indomitability with which one persists in striving for a goal beyond human reach. Wordsworth put it, in a visionary moment:

> Our destiny, our nature, and our home
> Is with infinitude—and only there;
> With hope it is, hope that can never die,
> Effort, and expectation, and desire,
> And something evermore about to be.[16]

Instead, in Nievo and Verga a prevailing mood is of resignation or despair—a hopeless nostalgia for a sheltered place that, though unforgotten, is forever gone. Luperini makes the further point that in Verga's later fiction, the notion of an original place of security and community is represented as having become an illusion in the modern world with the result that the *peregrinatio vitae*, in the lack of an origin as well as of an end, can no longer serve its age-old function of endowing human life with structure, meaning, and value. For such a view, as Luperini says, the most authentic image for life is not a journey, but (in the title of Verga's collection of short stories in 1901) *Vagabondaggio*—a random wandering without direction or destination.

The sentiment that life lacks either design or meaning, however widespread in the literature of the present century, by no means marks the end of the literary use of the image of life as a journey. It was more than a decade after the death of Giovanni Verga in 1922 that T. S. Eliot published his *Four Quartets* (1935– 42), which is the most sustained and intricate deployment of the motif in all of literature. The whole of Eliot's long poem articulates a figurative quest, by land and sea and underground, for a garden, "our first world," that has been glimpsed and lost but not forgotten. That the journey is circular is indicated by the persistent and paradoxical interplay, in the course of the poem, between the words *beginning* and *end*; and the second quartet, "East Coker," itself enacts the circular shape by opening "In my beginning is my end" and by closing with the repetition of the opening sentence, with its elements reversed: "In my end is my beginning." We learn that this movement signifies the poet's own educational journey, which (as in Wordsworth's *Prelude*) constitutes a dual education, both in his life and in his poetic craft; and in the traditional way, the place of origin, the unforgotten garden, is identified as home: "Home is where one starts from." This origin turns out also to have been the goal of the quest, for "the way forward is the way back";[17] although, as the end of the *Quartets* reveals, it is only when our circumnavigation has reached its haven that we will recognize that it has been, all along, our home:

> We shall not cease from exploration
> And the end of all our exploring
> Will be to arrive where we started
> And know the place for the first time.
> Through the unknown, remembered gate
> When the last of earth left to discover
> Is that which was the beginning.[18]

This is a remarkably inventive poem that, in the way it orders and relates its elements, eminently justifies its reputation as a distinctively modernist work. In those elements themselves, however, we can recognize the Romantic image of the educational journey impelled by a dialectic of contraries; and beyond that, the model of Dante's *Divine Comedy* that Eliot's poem often echoes and emulates; and ultimately, the Augustinian paradigm of the *peregrinatio vitae* as a quest whose goal is not in this world. Eliot's poem epitomizes the long and varied history of the topos of the spiritual journey, even as it attests its continuing viability as an imaginative option.

UGO FOSCOLO'S EUROPE: A JOURNEY FROM THE SUBLIME TO ROMANTIC HUMOR

Gustavo Costa

The concept of Europe envisioned by Ugo Foscolo was deeply affected by the aesthetic views that dominated his life. The idea of Europe is a reflection of his creative activity and as such it must be extrapolated from his works in prose and verse. These show a considerable variety of genres, corresponding to different psychological moods, which Foscolo translates into two opposite aesthetic values: the sublime and the comic. Both are linked to the theme of the journey, which can be either sublime (as in the case of Ulysses) or comic (as in the case of Sterne's Yorick). Travel projected into the mythic past of Greece belongs to the superior sphere of the sublime, which allows us to overcome the narrow confines of geography and history in order to live in an enchanted world where geographical distance and historical remoteness disappear in a kind of mystic embrace. But travel can also be a contemporary fact, imposed by practical necessities, and in this case, it is eminently comic. In this paper, I intend to show how Foscolo achieved the fusion of the sublime and the comic dimensions of travel literature in his fragmentary *Lettere scritte dall'Inghilterra* or *Gazzettino del Bel Mondo*, which he started at the beginning of 1817 and left unfinished in March 1818.[1] Foscolo undertook an artistic itinerary from the sublime to Romantic humor, which more or less mirrored his own journey from the Ionian Islands to Italy, and from there to England. Foscolo's Europe basically consisted of Greece, Italy, and England, viewed in a sublime or comic perspective, which at the end blend together in the humor pervading the *Lettere.*

In his *Ortis* (1802), Foscolo expressed his personal experience of exile from Venice and depicted Italy as a part of Europe exposed to political offenses, as well as to artistic models from northern countries. Among these, we should mention Goethe's *Werther* and Sterne's *Sentimental Journey.* The latter might have directed Foscolo's creative power toward a kind of Romantic humor, based on the coincidence of the sublime and the ludicrous. But it was not so, since the main component of *Ortis* appears to be Edmund Burke's identification of the sublime with terror and grief, as Cesarotti pointed out in a letter (which, incidentally, was grossly misinterpreted by Walter Binni).[2] In his lyric poem *Dei sepolcri* (1807), Foscolo views Italy as the equivalent of Greece and implicitly adopts an image of Europe in Graeco-Roman terms, perfectly suited to the Neoclassical taste of his times. What distinguishes *Dei sepolcri* from other Italian Neoclassical poems is its rigorous and original use of aesthetic principles, derived from the treatise *On the Sublime,* attributed to Longinus. Thanks to the inspiration drawn from Longinus (an author whom Foscolo, contrary to the majority of his contemporaries, was able to read in the original Greek text), the Italian poet was able to overcome the limits of time and space in the mystic union of great souls from different times and countries, which Longinus advocated in his treatise.[3]

In the unfinished *Le grazie,* Foscolo continued to cultivate an image of Europe consisting mainly of Greece and Italy. Such an image coincided with the triumph of the beautiful over the sublime, celebrated by Foscolo under the stimulus of Yves-Marie André, Raphael Mengs, and Johannes Winckelmann, in polemic with Burke's and Mendelssohn's aesthetic theories, as appears from Foscolo's "Dissertation on an Ancient Hymn to the Graces" (1822): "If, instead of their poets furnishing subjects, attitudes, and expressions, the Athenians had possessed philosophers like Burke and Mendelssohn, it may be doubted, whether they would ever have executed those masterpieces of sculpture,

A. Appiani. *Ritratto di Ugo Foscolo* (Portrait of Ugo Foscolo). Ca. 1802. Oil on canvas, 88 x 72 cm. Pinacoteca di Brera, Milan.

which Phidias acknowledges he copied from three lines of the *Iliad*."[4]

Paradoxically, Foscolo's disenchantment with the contemporary aesthetics of the sublime was itself a development of the treatise *On the Sublime* 14.2, where Longinus stresses the role of great models in the creative process:

> Still more effectual will it be to suggest this question to our thoughts, "What sort of hearing would Homer, had he been present, or Demosthenes have given to this or that when said by me, or how would they have been affected by the other?" For the ordeal is indeed a severe one, if we presuppose such a tribunal and theatre for our own utterances, and imagine that we are undergoing a scrutiny of our writings before these great heroes, acting as judges and witnesses.[5]

This passage was considered highly significant by Foscolo, as appears from his essay entitled "Traduzione de' due primi canti dell'*Odissea* di Ippolito Pindemonte" (1810), where Foscolo paraphrased and lauded Longinus's preference for a public composed exclusively of dead, but outstanding writers:

> "Immaginate che Demostene, Socrate e Omero leggano quanto scrivete": questo è il piú bel precetto della letteratura; trovasi con altri pochissimi d'egual tempra nel libro *Del Sublime* di Dionisio Longino, dal quale, malgrado le magnificenze che se ne cantano, potrebbesi estrarre quattro pagine, inciderle in bronzo, o piuttosto trascriverle in lettere cubitali su le quattro pareti di tutte le scuole di eloquenza, e poi confinare il resto di quel trattato tra le inezie e le noie rettoriche.

> ["Imagine that Demosthenes, Socrates, and Homer are reading what you write": this is the most beautiful precept of literature; taking its place among few others of equal quality in the book *On the Sublime* by Dionysus Longinus, from which despite the praise people accord it, you can extract four pages, inscribe them in bronze, or rather tran-

scribe them in huge letters on the four walls of all the schools of eloquence, and then throw away the rest of that treatise with other trifles and annoyances of rhetoric.]⁶

Foscolo's idiosyncratic sublime offered a highly sophisticated motivation to his snobbish attitude toward contemporary culture, which being the opposite of the sublime, could be expressed only in comic terms. It is no wonder that the *Lettere*, conceived as a mirror of contemporary life, are intrinsically comic even when dealing with the sublime itself. A case in point is the following passage from the so-called *Della poesia moderna*, where Foscolo inveighs against modern aestheticians:

> Fu ed è moda che i professori di metafisica francesi, inglesi e tedeschi insegnassero belle arti. Mengs diede precetti ed esempi a dipingere metafisicamente. Le nostre Accademie dissertano intorno al *Bello*; alla *Grazia*; al *Sublime:* teorie ignote all'età di Raffaello, del Correggio e di Michelangelo, i quali contemplavano le creazioni della natura con cuore non per anche gelato dalle speculazioni, e con mente vergine di sistemi. Ad essi bastava mostrare il *Come* sentivano e immaginavano la natura bella, sublime, e graziosa; or tutti vogliamo trovare il *Perché*.
>
> [It used to be and still is the fashion for French, English, and German metaphysics professors to teach fine arts. Mengs gave precepts and examples of how to paint metaphysically. Our academies give dissertations on Beauty; Grace; the Sublime: theories unknown at the time of Raffaello, Correggio, Michelangelo, who contemplated the creations of nature with their hearts not at all frozen by speculations, and with minds free of systems. For them it was enough to show *How* they felt and imagined nature to be beautiful, sublime, and gracious; now we all want to find the *Why*.]⁷

Foscolo's impatience with the excessive theorizing of his own times—an impatience probably inspired by Giambattista Vico's philosophy, according to which artistic creativity (based on imagination) antedates the rules of the poetics (based on reflection)—reveals Foscolo's partiality for Italy, which he viewed as the center of European civilization, at the expense of France, England, and Germany. Yet, in deprecating the proliferation of sterile theories, Foscolo reflected an attitude quite common among his contemporaries, even in England, as appears from Byron's attack against Coleridge in the dedication of *Don Juan* (2.5–8): "And Coleridge too has lately taken wing, / But like a hawk encumbered with his hood, / Explaining metaphysics to the nation, / I wish he would explain his explanation."[8] As usual, despite his proclaimed hostility to modernity, Foscolo was on the same wavelength as that of the most relevant European authors. He sensed that the modern world, being absolutely unfit for the sublime, is ludicrous in all its manifestations, including its speculations on the sublime. For this reason, Foscolo adopted in his *Lettere* a highly original style, amalgamating the sublime and the comic, namely the nostalgia for the mythic past of Greece and Italy that continued to haunt him and his everyday experience of the petty problems connected with his condition of an expatriate in England. The result of Foscolo's creative efforts is an unfinished but fascinating work, that can be subsumed under the category of Romantic humor, namely the reverse of the sublime, according to Jean Paul Richter's *School of Aesthetics* (1804).[9]

Foscolo had meditated on Plutarch's essay *On Exile 2* (*Moralia*, 599), according to which expatriation is a matter of opinion to be viewed either as a calamity or as an advantage:

> It is by nature that stone is hard, it is by nature that ice is cold; it is not from outside themselves, fortuitously, that they convey the sensation of rigidity and freezing; but banishment, loss of fame, and loss of honors, like their opposites, crowns, public office, and front-seat privileges, whose measure of causing sorrow and joy is not their own nature, but our judgment, every one makes light or heavy for himself, and easy to bear or the reverse.[10]

Plutarch proves the validity of his statement, referring to two texts. The first one, drawn from Euripides's *The Phoenician Maidens* 388–89, contains Jocasta's question addressed to Polynices: "What is the loss of country? A great ill?" as well as Polynices's unequivocal answer: "The greatest; and no words can do it justice." The second text quoted by Plutarch is Alexander Aetolus's epigram, in which the poet Alcman expresses his satisfaction for having quit Lydia, his native country, in order to become a citizen of Sparta.[11] Foscolo did not ignore the exhilarating feeling of liberty that a foreign country can inspire in a traveler open to new experiences. Especially his early correspondence from England reveals (to put it in Mario Scotti's words) Foscolo's "sensazione gioiosa della riscoperta libertà."[12] Yet he decided to adopt Euripides's passage as an epigraph for the fragment of the *Lettere* entitled "Esilio" ("tornerò ad affliggermi degli altrui guai con Euripide allorché mi sarò con voi spassionato de' miei" [I shall go back to Euripides to concern myself with other people's troubles after I shall have vented my grief unto you]), leaving aside the gist of Plutarch's essay in which Euripides was quoted with Alexander Aetolus (the "opuscoli di Plutarco *De exilio* dov'è citato" [booklets by Plutarch *On Exile* where he is quoted]).[13] Obviously, Foscolo did not resist the temptation to give an excerpt of sublime poetry that could elevate the daily problems he faced as an exile.

However, it would be a mistake to view Foscolo's preference for Euripides as a mere literary gimmick. When he wrote "Esilio," Foscolo harbored the tragic foreboding that he would never be able to go back to Italy, as appears from the following passage, in which he refers to the period he spent in France (1804–6), while serving in Napoleon's army:

> E temo ch'io non riavrò il piacere di cui ho goduto quando ritornando dopo due anni rividi con occhi lacrimosi di gioia i miei libri, di piú gioia che non rividi gli amici miei.
>
> [And I am afraid I shall never have again the pleasure I felt when, coming back after two years, I saw my books again,

with tears of joy in my eyes, with more joy than when I saw my friends.]¹⁴

This premonition is almost hidden in a frivolous context, dealing with the partiality of English writers, such as Addison and Fielding, for epigraphs and quotations ("Gl'Inglesi ne sono pazzi come pure di citazioni" [The English are as crazy about them as they are about quotations]).¹⁵ The same feeling that is typical of "Esilio" can be found as well in all the drafts and notes that constitute the *Lettere*. The most striking characteristic of Foscolo's unfinished project is the tragic feeling that lies buried under the jocular surface of its sprightly prose. One of the most convincing expressions of the ubiquitous tension between tragedy and comedy is to be found in the introductory letter that Foscolo completed on 25 December 1817:

> E appunto perché sull'Inghilterra io scriveva, per cosí dir, novellando; e intanto nella mia memoria risanguinavano piaghe—per le quali il forte sdegna di lasciare udire lamenti; e il cittadino vorrebbe poterle palliare; né io bramava che di sfogarmi secretamente—io allora non m'intendeva, o lettore, che tu pure dovessi essere depositario delle lettere mie.

> [And precisely because, when I was writing about England, I was fictionalizing, so to speak; but in the meantime in my memory wounds had started to bleed again—and while the strong disdain to let their moans be heard, and the average person wishes to alleviate the pain, I only longed to give vent to them secretly—so I did not mean, oh reader, that you should also be the trustee of these letters of mine.]¹⁶

Apart from the conventional disclaimer of fictitious epistolary works, allegedly written for private consumption, what we have here is an accurate description of the two main ingredients of the *Lettere:* tragedy and comedy. These basic components exert upon each other a strong magnetic pull, which precludes the possibility of a purely sublime or comic expression. The ultimate result of those opposite drives is Romantic humor. In his *Lettere*, Foscolo experimented with a style that was highly appreciated in northern Europe, especially in England. From this point of view, Foscolo's physical journey to England appears to have been also an artistic evolution toward Romantic humor.

Such an evolution was the fruit of a laborious gestation, strongly influenced by Sterne, whose *Sentimental Journey* Foscolo translated into Italian from the original, while he was in France in 1805. As appears from his *Notizia intorno a Didimo Chierico* (1816), Foscolo discovered in Sterne's novels a "nuova specie d'ironia, non epigrammatica, né suasoria, ma candidamente ed affettuosamente storica" [a new kind of irony which was neither epigrammatic nor persuasive, but simply and warmly historical].[17] In the dedication of the second edition of his *Tristram Shandy* (1760), Sterne asserted that "every time a man smiles,—but much more so, when he laughs, it adds something to his Fragment of Life."[18] But Foscolo was perfectly aware that Sterne's magic style was made not only of mirth but also of tears ("ma pare ch'egli inoltre sapesse che ogni lagrima insegna a' mortali una verità" [But it seems he also knew that every tear teaches mortals a truth]).[19] Certainly, Sterne's new brand of narrative irony suggested to Foscolo a new aesthetic possibility, resulting from the blend of tragedy and comedy. Sterne's artistic vision was founded on a subversion of traditional rhetoric, which had separated the sublime from the ludicrous, as appears from *Tristram Shandy* I, chapter 19, where the eloquence of Tristram's father is jocularly described as a natural gift: "Persuasion hung upon his lips. . . . And yet, 'tis strange he had never read Cicero nor Quintilian's *De oratore*, nor Isocrates, nor Aristotle, nor Longinus amongst the ancients."[20] The taste was decidedly changing, since Longinus himself, whom Pope viewed as the perfect embodiment of the sublime, could be quoted in order to poke fun at the admirers of ancient rhetoric.[21] Such a desecrating attitude, which paved the way for modern aesthetics, based on Romantic humor, was not ignored in the Venetian literary world, where a brilliant novelist such as Francesco Gritti, in his *La mia istoria ovvero Memorie del Signor Tommasino* (1767–68), could satirize a speech for its Longinian character ("la mia irresistibile forza de' miei sillogismi pieni zeppi di verità e della più fina quintessenza del gran Longino" [the irresistable strength of my syllogisms crammed full of truth and of the subtle quintessence of the great Longinus]).[22]

However, the most accomplished example of Romantic humor that Italian literature could offer Foscolo was Alfieri's *Vita*, an autobiography published in 1806 that was also a travel book dealing with various countries of Europe.[23] In a fragment of his *Lettere*, Foscolo epitomizes in a few lines the content of Alfieri's *Vita*, calling attention to some revealing episodes:

> L'Alfieri incocciatosi che il cavallo saltasse una sbarra nell'Hyde Park si slogò un braccio, e dopo tre o quattro giorni duellò—poi tornato a Firenze vestiva da militare perché parevagli farsi piú bello—poi scrisse tragedie e abbellì la poesia italiana dell'unica corona che le mancava.
>
> [Alfieri was so determined to make his horse jump a barrier in Hyde Park that he dislocated an arm, and after three or four days fought a duel—then went back to Florence dressed in military garb because he thought it made him more handsome—then he wrote tragedies and endowed Italian poetry with the only crown it had been missing.][24]

Foscolo, who liked to view himself as Alfieri's heir, alludes to his *Vita*, part 1, epoch 3, chapter 10, which contains a romanesque description of Alfieri's adventures during his second stay in England, namely his love affair with Penelope Pitt. Such adventures included a terrible fall, which took place as Alfieri, mounted on a good horse, attempted to jump a gate. As a consequence of this accident, Alfieri's left shoulder was dislocated. In spite of this injury, Alfieri was able to fight a duel with his mistress's jealous husband who had discovered their adulterous affair.[25] Alfieri's fall from his horse suggested to Foscolo a self-serving comparison with a similar accident he had on 25 July 1817 ("non voglio spedire domani il precedente numero senza questo, tanto da non lasciarvi fantasticare cos'abbia a che fare l'Alfieri con la tribolazione della mia gamba" [I do not want to mail the preceding issue tomorrow without the current one, lest you should speculate about what Alfieri had to do with my leg injury]).²⁶ In one of his letters, addressed to John Allen on 2 September 1817, Foscolo related his own fall from a horse, which, after immobilizing him for three weeks, left him with a limp. Even in this account, one can notice the same tension between the sublime and the ludicrous that pervades the *Lettere*, since Foscolo—after comparing himself to Theseus as described in Virgil's *Aeneid* 6.618–19 and to Philoctetes, the hero of one of Sophocles's tragedies—does not hesitate to identify himself with the antihero of Cervantes's *Don Quijote*:

> Le chirurgien m'a tenue dans l'immobilité du Héros Theseus pendant vingt et un jours: *aeternumque sedebat—Infelix Theseus—*: maintenant je suis le Héros Filoctetes; je marche boiteux comme lui; et la nuit je pousse des cris aussi aigus que les siens: car le rhumatisme n'a point *declined the occasion*—et je finirai par devenir la véritable figure du Héros Don Quixote mon ami, et, je crois, l'un de mes ancêtres.
>
> [The surgeon immobilized me like Hero Theseus for twenty-one days: *forever stood still—Unhappy Theseus—*: now I am the Hero Philoctetes; I walk with a limp like he does; and at night I let out cries as piercing as his; because the rheumatism has not at all *declined the occasion*—and I shall end up by becoming a veritable Hero Don Quixote, my friend and, I believe, one of my ancestors.]²⁷

In the above passage from the *Lettere*, Foscolo alludes also to another episode from Alfieri's autobiography, which is an excellent example of Romantic humor. In *Vita*, part 1, epoch 4, chapter 3, Alfieri confessed that, at the very time he was writing his *Virginia* and his essay *Della tirannide*, he was still wearing the uniform of the Sardinian army, simply because he wanted to look smarter and more attractive. Commenting on his own vanity, Alfieri made the striking discovery of the dual nature of his own character, consisting of a giant and a dwarf: "In questa particolarità ... si scorgerà da chi ben osserva e riflette, che talvolta l'uomo, o almeno, che io riuniva in me, per cosí dire, il gigante ed il nano" [In this instance, those who observe well and reflect clearly, will realize that sometimes man (or at least I) combines within him the giant and the dwarf].[28] Such a confession points to the same tension between the sublime and the ludicrous that Foscolo experienced in himself and that he expressed in his writings. It was a tension that polarized the contradictions of Foscolo's personality, reflecting an essential condition of the Romantic malaise. Just as Alfieri discovered he had a split character, which allowed him to be a giant and a dwarf at the same time, so too did Foscolo realize that he could at once be Ortis and Didimo Chierico. While Ortis represented the traveler journeying in the mythic dimension of the sublime, Didimo Chierico represented the traveler journeying in the contemporary world, who had seen many countries, described them in his autobiography composed in Greek, and yet regretted having seen them ("parla de' molti paesi da lui veduti, e si pente d'averli veduti" [He speaks of the many countries he has seen, and how he regrets having seen them]), as Foscolo stated in his *Notizia*.[29] Didimo was also the fictitious author of the *Hypercalypsis* (1816), a vitriolic attack against Urbano Lampredi, where Foscolo depicts himself in the larger-than-life figure of the "vir militaris" [man of arms], who, having played the role of the archangel, in the end proclaims to be just a cavalry captain ("non sum apostolus nec propheta nec angelus, sed centurio Draconum" [I am not an aspostle nor a prophet nor an angel, but a Draconian centurion]).[30] Indeed, Didimo, like Foscolo himself, was a rationalist who paradoxically believed in the power of prophecy ("Credeva nell'ispirazione profetica, anzi presumeva di saperne le fonti" [He believed in prophetic inspiration, as a matter of fact, he presumed to know its sources]).[31] In his *Lettere,* Foscolo does not fail to mention Didimo, who was well informed of the ways of the world thanks to his travels to Europe. In his *Lettera sulla moda* where he deals with the habit of kissing ladies' hands, a habit that did not exist in England, Foscolo fondly evokes Didimo: "ma qui si tratta del nostro secolo, di mode e di baci—e tu sí Didimo Chierico, amico mio! tu ne sapevi piú d'Anacreonte" [But here we are speaking about our century, about fashions and kisses—and you of all people Didimo Chierico, my friend! You knew more about them than Anacreontes]).[32] As he had already done in his *Notizia,* Foscolo feigns to have lost track of Didimo ("poi non l'abbiamo veduto piú: né so s'egli cammini ancora sopra la terra" [we have never seen him since: and I do not even know if he still walks this earth]).[33] In a discarded draft of the same *Lettera sulla moda,* Foscolo describes Didimo's gift of prophecy and mentions his own *Hypercalypsis:* "E' fu nella sua adolescenza invasato da uno spirito o demone di profezia, e scrisse certo libretto a modo della Scrittura che si chiama con vocabolo strano *Hypercalypsis"* [He was in his adolescence possessed by a spirit or demon or prophecy, and he wrote a certain booklet styled after the Scriptures with the strange title of *Hypercalypsis*].[34] Then Foscolo refers to chapter 17 of the prophetic work he attributed to Didimo, who allegedly exposed the misery of Paris, Rome, and Milan, the three Babylons of Napoleonic Europe: "ei pronostica di tre Babilonie—Babilonia massima, Babilonia perpetua, e Babilonia minima [He predicts three Babylons—Babylon major, Babylon perpetual, and Babylon minor].[35] Since the *Lettere* were intended for English readers, Foscolo found it expedient to overlook the fact that Didimo, in *Hypercalypsis* 17.9, had directed his barbs against England, the rich Babylon, and had predicted its ruin ("ad te quoque perveniet calix: inebriaberis atque nudaberis" [and the chalice will reach you too: you will be inebriated and laid bare]).[36] However, Didimo's negative view of England did not cease to affect Foscolo's direct experience of English life, as appears from his correspondence. In the letter addressed to Quirina Mocenni Magiotti on 20 February 1818, Foscolo criticized the materialistic mentality of England for its glorification of money:

> E t'ho già avvertito, credo, che qui la povertà è vergogna che nessun merito lava. È delitto non punito dalle leggi, ma perseguitato piú crudelmente dal mondo. Sí fatto modo di pensare fa di grandi beni alla nazione—ma riduce chi ha bisogno a non potere cercare né aiuto, né sfogo.
>
> [And I have already warned you, I believe, that here poverty is the shame no merit washes away. It is a crime not punished by law, but it is persecuted even more cruelly by society. Such way of thinking brings great benefit to the nation—but diminishes those in need to the point where they are unable to seek help or relief.][37]

After his initial enthusiasm, Foscolo made the upsetting discovery that, being an Italian writer, he could not prosper in England, where the Italian language was generally ignored. In the same letter to Quirina, Foscolo lamented that he was unable to write in English and, forgetting Didimo's alleged aloofness about financial matters, regretted the good money he could have made as an English writer, thanks to the reputation he already enjoyed as an Italian author:

> Questa Fama che non viene meritamente, ma che pure mi è data, m'arricchirebbe, se potessi scrivere Inglese;—ma chi intende il mio Italiano? ... Moltissimi lo studiano, pochi l'imparano: tutti affettano o presumono di saperlo. Ma i libraji assicurano che appena d'un libro Italiano, anche classico, si vendono cinquecento copie in tre anni;—e d'un libro Inglese, d'autore di qualche nome, se ne vendono cinque e spesso sei mila copie in due o tre settimane.
>
> [This Fame that does not come from merit, but is nonetheless given me, would make me rich, if I could write in

English;—but who understands my Italian? . . . Many study it, few learn it: everyone affects it or presumes to know it. But the booksellers estimate that an Italian book, even a classic, can sell scarcely five hundred copies in three years;—and an English book, no matter what the author's name, will sell five or often six thousand copies in two or three weeks.]³⁸

England offered Foscolo a unique opportunity to acquire a firsthand knowledge of a modern, growing literary life, supported by a thriving book market, all of which was a far cry from the stagnating situation in Italy, where men of letters who could not count on their own private fortunes were still obliged to make a living by soliciting state patronage or private support. A fragment of the *Lettere* shows that Foscolo had grasped the interconnection between an affluent society and a vigorous culture, since he stresses the fact that a reading public is a function of leisure, money, and self-love: "La Lettura viene da' costumi—perché per essi s'ha tempo di Leggere—dal danaro perché s'ha mezzo d'incivilirsi, e spendere—dalla vanità perché provoca emulazione" [Reading comes from customs—because they give you time to read—from money because it gives you the means to spend and to become civilized—from vanity because it brings about emulation].³⁹ Since English literature was financed by the entire nation through the publishers, the English poets were much less prone to adulation than their Italian counterparts, who could not rely upon a vast audience:

> Quanto a' poeti inglesi sono tutti meno adulatori perché son piú liberi degli italiani;—ma perché sono poeti si compiacciono anch'essi del favore de' grandi; oggi peraltro men che mai perché i lor cari mecenati sono i libraji, e quindi l'intera nazione.
>
> [As to the English poets, they are less prone to lavish flattery because they are freer than the Italians; but because they are poets, they too take pleasure in receiving favors from

the powerful; today, however, they are less inclined to do so because not only booksellers but the entire nation have become their dear patrons.]⁴⁰

In light of his English experience, Foscolo did not hesitate to manifest, once again, his profound distaste for Italian literary life, which was not founded on a national community since the very idea of country was stifled first by the Napoleonic regime and then by the Restoration sanctioned by the Congress of Vienna:

> Or da quattr'anni ogni speranza di patria dileguasi; gl'ingegni frementi sotto Napoleone si giacciono in muta costernazione; e coloro che scrivono per venalità o per vanità, non hanno altra suppellettile che di parole; e combattono fra di loro: gli uni, ad immiserire con grammaticali superstizioni la lingua—gli altri a snaturarla con formule matematiche, o con vocaboli metafisici che inorgogliscono l'intelletto e confondono l'evidenza delle idee; stile de' romanzieri, de' poeti, e degli storici d'oggi, avvampante d'entusiasmo e di passioni artefatte.

> [In the last four years, every hope for the homeland has vanished; talents that were vibrant under Napoleon are now prostrate in silent consternation; and those who write, for money or for vanity, have no other resource but words, and they fight among themselves; some to impoverish language with pedantic niceties; others to distort it with mathematical formulas, or with metaphysical terms that elate the intellect and cloud the expression of ideas; such is the style of today's novelists, poets, historians, flaring up with enthusiasm and with artificial passions.]⁴¹

Here Didimo's comic dislike for the literary quarrels of Italy, which he defined as eunuchs' battles ("l'ho imparato appunto da Didimo che i duelli di penna s'hanno da chiamare *eunucomachie*" [I learned it in fact from Didimo, that these penned duels really ought to be called eunuch-fights])⁴² goes hand in hand with

Ortis's tragic grief for the loss of country, which is expressed in the sublime opening of Foscolo's novel: "Il sacrificio della patria nostra è consumato: tutto è perduto; e la vita, se pure ne verrà concessa, non ci resterà che per piangere le nostre sciagure e la nostra infamia" [The death of our country has taken place; everything is lost; and all that will be left for us, if indeed we are allowed to live, is to lament our misfortune and our disgrace].⁴³ Foscolo's Europe consisted of highly diversified nations, which he naturalistically regarded as representing different species of men, more adept than other living creatures at loving and killing each other:

> La genetrice Natura sa bene quali diverse doti e dosi bisognino meglio a tutti noi sue creature uomini e bestie. E quanto agli animali umani destinati da lei ad amarsi piú ch'altri fra loro e a trucidarsi piú ch'altri, essa gli ha divisi in *specie*—e che noi diciamo *Nazioni*—ed ha provveduto ciascheduna di loro dell'istinto piú acconcio all'intento dell'amarsi e del trucidarsi.
>
> [Mother Nature well knows which diverse gifts, and how many of them, are most necessary for all of us her creatures, men and beasts. And as for human animals, destined by her to love each other more than others and to kill each other more than others, she has divided them into *species*—which we call *Nations*—and has provided each one of them with the instincts most suitable to loving and killing.]⁴⁴

Yet Europe was held together by a kind of bonding cement, namely Western civilization, while the non-European peoples constituted the barbarian world. This eurocentric view, universally accepted in Foscolo's time, was never rejected by him, although he was somewhat uneasy about it.

Thanks to his familiarity with Vico's *Scienza Nuova*,⁴⁵ Foscolo was aware that the notions of barbarism and civilization are relative, in as much as they represent different stages of the historical development of all nations, including those of Europe.

This relativistic view of the opposition between barbarism and civilization invited comparisons of European and non-European peoples in order to better understand the history of Europe itself, from its origins to the present. Such is the proper perspective that helps us understand Foscolo's observations on the inability of both barbarians and civilized men to think, when they reach the apotheosis of barbarism and civilization. According to Foscolo, barbarians tend to fix their attention on very few objects, while civilized people tend to disperse their intellectual powers over a wide range of subject matter. Therefore, barbarians are comparable to maniacs, while civilized men are to be considered fatuous:

> Parmi che nel sommo della barbarie o della civiltà de' popoli la facoltà di pensare è inattiva. I barbari, per troppa intensità di passione verso pochissimi oggetti potrebbero paragonarsi ai *Maniaci*—e noi, per troppa distrazione a infiniti capricci, siam simili a' *Fatui*.
>
> [It seems to me that nations, when at the height of their barbarity or their civilization, lose their faculty to think. The barbarians, because of their strong passion for very few objects, could be likened to *Maniacs*—we, on the other hand, distracted by two many whims, are similar to *Fools*.][46]

Can Europe, the domain of fatuousness, boast of its alleged superiority over the uncivilized nations characterized by mania? It is difficult to say. Foscolo limits himself to assert that mania is the result of an excess of feelings and can be cured, while nobody can recover from fatuousness, although the latter is highly appreciated in the fashionable world: "Notate che la *Mania* deriva dal troppo sentire; però è men difficile a guarire; ma è malinconica. La *Fatuità* non ha piú forze da riaversi in salute; ma perché è spensierata ed allegra piace al *Bel mondo* [Note that *Mania* springs from feeling too obsessively; however, it is not very difficult to recover from it; but it is melancholic. From *Fatuousness* one does not heal; but because it is lighthearted and cheerful it pleases *High Society*].[47] The dilemma between barbarism or mania and civilization or fatuousness has not only a geographical but also a literary and critical dimension. Foscolo believes that the Muslims who read only the Koran are no more afflicted by mania than those European critics who extol Homer or Dante over all other authors: "I Dervisci e i Monaci d'ogni setta i quali non hanno libro se non il loro Alcorano, e parimenti i settari d'Omero e di Dante che infuriano contro gli autori d'ogni secolo e popolo, non son forse *Maniaci*?" [The Dervishes and Monks of every sect who have no other books but their Koran, like the sectarians of Homer and Dante who inveigh against the writers of every century and every people, are they not perhaps *Maniacs*?].[48] Foscolo did not want to be a maniac. Like Didimo who liked to read all sorts of books ("Leggeva quanti libri gli capitavano" [He read every book that came his way]).[49] Foscolo was familiar with an impressive number of European authors, as appears from the drafts of his *Lettere*. Yet he also felt that we should not be inclined to admire all novelties, because such an attitude generates skepticism:

> Frattanto noi correndo dietro la turba tumultuosa degli scrittori, combattiamo per conquistare un'infinità d'opinioni e di fantasia e di novità, finché ciascheduno di noi volendole afferrar tutte quante, si stanca, s'annoia di tutte e cade smemorato sul campo di battaglia del *Pirronismo*.
>
> [Meanwhile we, running after the tumultuous rabble of writers, we fight to conquer an endless number of opinions and of fantasies and of novelties, until every single one of us, wanting to grab hold of all of them, gets tired, gets bored with it all, and falls senseless on the battlefield of Pyrrhonism.][50]

Echoing what Longinus maintains in his treatise *On the Sublime* 14.2, Foscolo once again stresses the importance of the great models, both ancient and modern, that enable us to think and, in this way, help us avoid the dangers of mania and fatuousness:

Adunque è da presumersi men barbaro quel *Bel mondo* popolato di scrittori e lettori i quali, studiando i pochi grandi esemplari d'ogni generazione fino alla nostra, possono educarsi a pensare; e quindi, a scansare gli inconvenienti della *Mania* e della *Fatuità*.

[Consequently, we can assume that the High society full of writers and literati is less uncivilized, as they study the few great examples of each generation up until ours and can educate themselves to think, and thus, shun the drawbacks of *Mania* and *Fatuousness*.][51]

According to Foscolo, if we follow his advice to converse only with major writers, whom Longinus did not hesitate to call "great heroes"[52] we will glean three essential principles: the general ideas of Truth and Beauty, as well as a more adequate idea of Taste. This aesthetic view, which adhered to Longinus's notion of the heroic, allowed Foscolo to replace the sublime with the beautiful and served as his antidote to the growing influence of German philosophy ("la Metafisica tedesca rivestita delle gonnelle di Madame di Staël" [German Metaphysics dressed up in the pettycoats of Madame de Staël]).[53] Obviously, Foscolo's artistic itinerary from the sublime to Romantic humor made him ready to complete *Le Grazie,* the magnum opus mentioned in a fragment of the *Lettere:*

Un amico mio di cui forse un giorno manderò a voi . . . un poema intitolato *Alle Grazie* scrive che le Grazie ebbero da Pallade in dono un velo che era istoriato a ricami di alcune pitture della vita umana.

[A friend of mine, whose poem entitled *Alle Grazie* I may one day send you, writes that, the Graces received as a gift from Pallas a veil embroidered and decorated with pictures of human life.][54]

Unfortunately, the financial problems Foscolo had to face in England prevented him from finding the poetic masterpiece he had been seeking throughout his lifetime.

THE ITALIAN JOURNEY: FROM JAMES TO ELIOT TO BROWNING

Eleanor Cook

My title has nothing to do with Goethe's Italian journey, except insofar as that famous tour of Italy was an educational journey, a *Bildungsreise*. I am interested in the Italian journey in Henry James's novel *Portrait of a Lady*, first published in 1881. I am also interested in the Italian journey in a second sense, the journey that James took back to George Eliot's novel *Daniel Deronda* (1876), and then back to what I think he saw there: Browning's famous dramatic monologue "My Last Duchess," published in 1842. Hence my title From James to Eliot to Browning, which follows a journey backward, a metalepsis. My general argument is that the journey to Italy is a unique type of *Bildungsreise*, to judge from James and Browning, two examples drawn from an English-language and (loosely speaking) a Protestant tradition. I shall start by outlining the argument for a line of succession from James back through Eliot to Browning. The James-Eliot journey is familiar enough: after all, James himself drew a map linking his novel with *Daniel Deronda*. The Browning link is new. I want then to offer some implications of this argument for our reading of James's novel, for different areas of criticism, and especially for our sense of the journey as *Bildungsreise*.

Briefly, a few facts. Browning and Eliot were of an age, James a generation younger. The paths of all three crossed in England, though casually. They met at dinners, or the younger man called on the eminent novelist. All three traveled in Italy; Browning and James lived there for protracted periods, Browning for all fifteen years of his married life, from 1846 to 1861. James spent an idyllic year in Rome from 1872 to 1873: "to the Villa Madama, on the side of Monte Mario; a place like a page out of Browning, wonderful in its haunting melancholy. The days follow each other in gentle variety, each one leaving me a little more *Roman* than before."[1] He wrote travel literature, including a volume called *Roman Rides*. He wrote much of *Portrait of a Lady* in Florence and Venice. Browning's knowledge of Italy was extensive, and he loved the country: "Open my heart and you will see, / Graved inside of it, 'Italy.'" Or: "Oh woman-country, wooed not wed, / Loved all the more by earth's male-lands." Many of his best, and best-known, poems are set in Italy and are spoken by Italian characters, sometimes historical: "The Bishop Orders His Tomb at St. Praxed's," "Andrea del Sarto," "Fra Lippo Lippi."[2] By 1881, much of Browning's poetry and all of Eliot's fiction were widely read and some commonly known. Certainly, James knew his Browning, both the man and the work. Impressions of the man provided James with a riddle that turned into the short story, "A Private Life." And James's characters read Browning. I offer this little compendium in order to show that a line of succession, James back through Eliot to Browning, is historically quite possible. I offer it also because I want to argue that hearing Browning's poem in James's novel opens a door for us back out into Italy as the setting and even the goal of Isabel Archer's tragic educational journey.

Let me now set before you three characters from these three works, two of whom live in Italy and one of whom, though he does not live there, dies there. All three are villains that we can fully enjoy detesting. They are Browning's Duke of Ferrara, Eliot's Mallinger Grandcourt, and James's Osmond, three brothers under the skin. One is Italian and noble; one is English and not noble; one is American and wishes he were noble. The chief interest of all three lies in their relation to the women they marry, three quite different women: the Duchess, Gwendolen

Harleth, and Isabel Archer. Two of these women, those in the novels, start or accomplish a *Bildungsreise* or educational journey, and for both a crisis and culmination occurs in Italy. For James's heroine, Isabel Archer, this not only occurs in Italy, it belongs to Italy, just as Browning's monologue not only occurs in Italy but also belongs to Italy.

We might briefly compare these three men, treating them as characters in the usual mimetic sense and reading synchronically. All three assume that they will rule over their intimates, and all three have a fastidious distaste for direct argument. We can hear the force of Browning's word "stoop" in his poem, especially when it is repeated: "E'en then would be some stooping; and I choose / Never to stoop." (The enjambment emphasizes the word "never," and so does the stress of the trochee in the word "never," where we expect a regular iambic foot.) The fastidious distaste for argument is also found in Eliot's Grandcourt and in James's Osmond: "In general, there was nothing he hated more than to be forced into anything like violence even in words: his will must impose itself without trouble" (*Daniel Deronda*, p. 396).

All three men perform for an audience, more or less consciously. David Shaw has drawn our attention to the Duke's monologue as theatrical performance, with the Duke as chief actor and also as director.[3] It is the Duke who controls the raising and the falling of the curtain over his now safely contained last wife. The same with Grandcourt. And the same with Osmond. Isabel is horrified to realize that Osmond, so apparently disdainful of popular opinion, actually lives by it: "It is true that Grandcourt went about with the sense that he did not care a languid curse for anyone's admiration: but this state of not-caring . . . required its related object—namely, a world of admiring or envying spectators: for if you are fond of looking stonily at smiling persons, the persons must be there and they must smile" (*Daniel Deronda*, p. 646).

Finally, all three are connoisseurs of sorts, with a highly developed aesthetic sensibility, whatever might be said of their moral sensibility. They choose their wives as part of their collections, so to speak. The Duke's former Duchess is now a proper object, a painting, to be admired as the flesh-and-blood woman could not be. The Duke's closing lines, as critics regularly note, appropriately point to another art object, a rarity that also tells a story of taming. The allegorical lesson to be read by the next wife is clear. Eliot's Grandcourt is a connoisseur of horses, and he thinks of Gwendolen in those terms. As for James's character, Gilbert Osmond, his reflections on Isabel as object are well known: "He thought Miss Archer sometimes of too precipitate a readiness. It was a pity she had that fault, because if she had not had it she really would have had none; she would have been as smooth to his general need of her as handled ivory to the palm. . . . She saw . . . the dry staring fact that she had been an applied handled hung-up tool, as senseless and convenient as mere shaped wood and iron" (*Portrait of a Lady*, pp. 259, 459).

I think this threefold confluence of villainy is no accident. To begin with George Eliot: Surely we ought to take heed when a friend of Deronda's, and a painter at that, regularly calls Gwendolen "the Duchess" and her husband, "the Duke." Her title is used sixteen times and his five times by my count. She is known as the Vandyk duchess; her husband as Duke Alfonso, the last husband of Lucrezia Borgia—as it happens, Duke Alfonso of Ferrara and the grandfather of the Duke Alfonso who is Browning's model for his Duke. Further, Eliot opens the death chapter, which is set in Italy, with Dante's story of a dissatisfied husband whose wife mysteriously disappears, the story of Madonna Pia. Or the supposed story, for it is disputed: the most familiar such story out of the annals of Italy, at least for a nineteenth-century English audience, would be Browning's story in "My Last Duchess." (To my knowledge, no critic of Eliot has heard this; critics have been reminded of Browning's poem, but no more than reminded.)

In *Daniel Deronda*, Dante's story and Browning's poem suggest a topos of murderous domination, together with some sense of wicked Italianate husbands. And critics are fond of the word

Italianate when comparing Grandcourt and Osmond. But the Italianness of Eliot's novel as a whole functions only as one more type of foreignness. The Italian journey (or rather the Italian trip) in this novel may be a synecdoche for Gwendolen's pitiful educational journey and Deronda's heroic one, but it is episodic. Eliot's novel is centered on the question of what it means to be a Jew. If the hero is on a quest for a city, that city is Jerusalem and not Rome. For James's heroine, I think that city is Rome.

Some forty years ago, the critic F. R. Leavis asserted that "Osmond is Grandcourt."[4] It seems self-evident that we should extend this equation to three terms, and say "Osmond is Grandcourt is the Duke of Ferrara." James, I surmise, heard exactly what Eliot was doing with Browning, and he decided to do something more and different. In part, the different direction he takes is obvious. He centers his novel on the woman, whereas Eliot divides her novel, tracing two separate plot lines that come close but do not join the narratives of the main characters, Daniel Deronda and Gwendolen Harleth. James makes Isabel Archer fully the protagonist and the tragic heroine of his novel. The challenge, as he knows, is whether a young woman can fully sustain the center of interest in such a novel. His models, as he says, are the heroines of Shakespeare and of Eliot, but in his capacious imagination, there also hung, I think, the portrait of an Italian duchess. Portrait of a Lady, Portrait of a Duchess. "That's my last lady painted on the wall, / Looking as if she were alive. I call / That piece a wonder, now. . . ." We can almost hear Gilbert Osmond speaking these lines. Yet James does not want us to hear Osmond speak. He wants us to hear what Isabel has to say. If he were rewriting Browning's monologue, he would put it into the mouth of the Duchess.

He began (as he tells us in his preface) with a character, not with a plot. Around this character, as by magic, suddenly appeared an entire setting: other characters, places, travel—in short, everything to show this young woman affronting her destiny, everything that would best show what her character was. She would travel, and the question became What kind of journey would she take? She would quest, but how, and why?

Hearing Browning's Italian poem inspires us to watch more intently the shape of Isabel's journey. Critics describe Isabel's gradual movement toward fuller knowledge as a journey, but her outward journeying, apart from the obvious move from North America to Europe, is still insufficiently read. *Portrait of a Lady* is divided into two parts: the first begins in England, in the country home called Gardencourt. James will make his heroine repeat two formal types of educational journey, one or both of which can become a path to inner, spiritual knowledge. The first is the *Bildungsreise* in the conventional sense of the Grand Tour of Europe, which Isabel undertakes, having begun in the inauspicious setting of Albany, New York (like James himself). The second is the *Bildungsreise* in the conventional sense of a journey that leads toward marriage. James is at pains to foreground this second kind of journey toward self-knowlege, and also to suggest that this journey is no end in itself for Isabel. That is to say, both these formal types of journey are treated with a certain Jamesian irony. They will contribute to Isabel's longer journey, the questing that is her life, just as they contribute to Deronda's larger journey, the questing that is his life.

The first part of James's novel ends in anticipation of Isabel's marriage, following her educational journey to Europe and, crucially, to Italy, to Florence. The second part opens in Rome, some three years after her marriage, and it is there that Isabel experiences her true educational journey, though she does not actually travel until the closing trip back to Gardencourt, and (beyond the novel) her much disputed return to Italy. The culmination of her *Bildungsreise* is indeed enlightenment. It comes in the great recognition scene, in chapter 42, "obviously," said James, "the best thing in the book." Chapter 42 is explicitly a recognition scene, as we hear in the opening paragraph: "this had given her the start that accompanies unexpected recognition." The knowledge of self and others, the new recognition, is terrible and chastening for her. Northrop Frye argues that "romance, tragedy, irony, and comedy are all episodes in a total quest-myth."⁵ Isabel's educational journey is experiential, moving from innocence to experience, and I think James treats it as tragedy.

Hearing Browning's poem causes us also to notice the word "court" echoing in Eliot's name, "Mallinger Grand-court," and also in James's name for his English country house, "Gardencourt." "Garden" plays against "grand" as we are offered two possible attributes of a court: the effect is to heighten allegorical reading. Isabel is very clearly associated with gardens, and critics have remarked on James's fine garden scenes. But James is also a writer who values courtliness and courtesy, in the best sense of these words. So does his character, Isabel Archer. She ought also to be associated with courtliness and courtesy, in the best sense of these words. Browning's Duchess delights in simple natural things—in a garden world, as critics regularly note—whereas the Duke is possessed by a sterile aestheticism. James's compound name, Gardencourt, suggests that this country house combines the ideals of both garden and court. And indeed, life in that house, for all the small quotidian strains, does proceed on the basis of an ideal garden life and an ideal courtly life. It is in that light that the opening tea ceremony may retrospectively be read, as against our first reading of four o'clock tea as a merely agreeable and perhaps overesteemed English habit. (The archetypes of garden and court are too well known to need identifying.)

Eliot's name, Grandcourt, speaks for itself. As it happens, Grandcourt does not aspire to high courtly life, though he likes a handsome social position. It is James who understood the obsessive desires of vanity, the desire of Gilbert Osmond to be able to say and do what Browning's Duke says and does—especially to be able to speak of a "nine-hundred-years-old-name"; "He [Osmond] had never forgiven his star for not appointing him to an English dukedom" (p. 258). If one is not born to the purple or married to it, one can at least marry someone (Isabel) who has actually turned down what one most desires, and then marry off one's daughter to the nine-hundred-year-old name. If one's daughter draws back from such a glorious marriage, because she is inconveniently in love with someone else, one may do with her what Browning's Duke may have done with his inconvenient Duchess, sequester her in a convent.[6] James's novel is a portrait of a lady, not of a duchess. Browning's poem highlights the fact that Isabel could have been a lady in the titled sense of the word. She could have been Lady Warburton. The senses in which Isabel is and is not a lady are central to the novel. Too often, critics discuss the question of being a lady only in terms of nineteenth-century gentility, forgetting the great debates and ideals of *gentillesse* (gentility [see Chaucer] or courtesy [see Castiglione]). Isabel's standards of courtesy and courtliness are high. As with Browning's Duchess, they constitute part of her very self, and as with Browning's Duchess, they constitute a standing rebuke to the titled or would-be-titled husband: "She had a certain way of looking at life which he took as a personal offence" (p. 359); "It was a strange opposition of the like of which she had never dreamed—an opposition in which the vital principle of the one was a thing of contempt to the other" (p. 356).

Hearing Browning's poem in James's novel leads us toward all Browning's Italian poems and hence toward Browning's whole sense of Italy. This, to me, is by far its most important function. The poem thereby offers a much wider context in which to read James's novel. It suggests we pay more attention to Isabel's move from Gardencourt to Italy and back to Gardencourt. It suggests that James's preface to *Portrait of a Lady* opens deliberately rather than casually with a vivid description of Venice. It suggests that the move from Florence to Rome in the novel is also deliberate. The importance of James's Italian setting has been underestimated, because it is not foregrounded in this portrait of a lady, nor is it made picturesque. Yet James exploits his Italian setting as thoroughly as Browning did, and he knew his Italian setting. It is true that the focus is on the human drama—a general point made in criticism, but only a half-truth.

James's Italian setting, or rather Italianness, is essential to his novel. I have already noted the shape of Isabel's travels, from her parental home to her ideal home (Gardencourt) through Europe and, crucially, to Florence, where she is manipulated into meeting Gilbert Osmond. Then from her new home—not in Florence, but in Rome—desperately back to Gardencourt at the end, only to make a heroic return trip to Rome. We may map her responses to Italy, and the responses of others. We may watch her move from girlish admiration to an apprehension of Rome as a place where people have suffered. We may watch the ruins of Rome draw her toward them, as they drew James himself. It is possible to read Isabel's responses to Florence and to Rome as merely outward reflections of her interior spiritual journey. To a degree, this is fair enough. But it uses a simple inside-outside paradigm, and it blunts James's artistry. If we hear Browning's poem and, beyond that, remember Browning's Italy, we read much more fully. I shall offer only one small example and one large. The small example: Isabel takes a memorable ride in the Campagna, and James builds on his own personal knowledge, as we know from his travel essays, *Roman Rides*. He also builds on contemporary knowledge of Browning's poem, "Two in the Campagna"—a poem of estranged lovers. Isabel has read her Browning, just as she has read Milton and the Bible, and all three are used allusively by James.

To take a much larger example: "My Last Duchess" is not the only poem by Browning to exploit a tension between a fine aesthetic sense and a crude or nonexistent ethical sense. The paradox of exquisite sensibility toward works of art combined with callousness toward other human beings is perpetually fascinating. Such a paradox may be seen in certain figures of the Italian Renaissance, at least as they are commonly perceived. They become the extreme types through which we test our thinking about these matters. The possible tensions between the ethical and the aesthetic is at the heart of James's work, and it is one of the acute questions for Browning too. It is just this question that the Italian journey, the *Bildungsreise* to Italy, may raise. James's return to Browning is not only a return to a setting in Italy but also to one of the deepest questions that engaged Browning's imagination.

I want to end by pointing toward some implications of this general argument for four different senses of the journey and four different areas of criticism.

First, the allusive journey of a writer back through earlier writers, and the critical area of allusion and echo. (I am taking some liberties here with the preposition *in* in the title of this conference. Yet surely our sense of the journey in any literature must include somewhere the important literary journeys taken by writers.) I have traced one such journey, a journey from James back through Eliot to Browning. There is a good deal of interest nowadays in literary allusion: I am thinking especially of the work of John Hollander and Christopher Ricks.[7] Henry James's journey takes the shape of the figure known as metalepsis, for he takes a metaleptic leap backward, over Eliot to the poems she has echoed, and thereby finds a new way of moving forward. In our typologies of the journey, we should include a writer's own journey back through the literary country where earlier writers live.

Second (and again taking liberties with the preposition *in*), the journey of the reader, and the area of generic criticism. I have been puzzled why so obvious a parallel as Browning's "My Last Duchess" has not seriously entered the discussion of James's novel. Perhaps this is because, in our own reading journeys, we sometimes forget that the barriers we erect between the different genres—say, between poetry and prose fiction—ought to be adaptable folding screens and not concrete walls. James, after all, spoke of the novelist as a poet. This is true of other walls as well, for example the walls between different time periods, and between different national literatures. Writers themselves read omnivorously, and they try to take us on their reading journeys, providing clear signposts and well-swept paths. But sometimes we simply sit down on the side of the road and refuse to budge. James Merrill, the contemporary American poet, can even hear Browning in the cadences of James's prose: "though a lot of the sound of James is prose, can't one tell that he'd read Browning?"[8] Few readers have as good an ear as Merrill's, but we can at least read something of what our writers read. Otherwise, our typologies of the journey will be much impoverished.

Third, James's novel traces the journey of a woman and hence my reading bears on the area of feminist criticism. Isabel Archer's journey from innocence to experience raises a question about the *Bildungsreise*. Is it different for a woman, and if so, always or sometimes? How far does a woman's educational journey begin after marriage, if she does marry, and what does this do to the typology of the educational journey? Should we say that women often have two educational journeys, and not one? How far is a woman's educational journey always contingent?

As an experiment, suppose we follow M. H. Abrams's fine mapping of a recurrent pattern in the German educational journey but alter the male words to female (always a useful exercise). Does the educational journey still sound right, and if not, why not?

> This process is represented in the plot-form of an educational journey in quest of a masculine other, whose mysterious attraction compels the protagonist to abandon her childhood sweetheart and the simple security of home and family (equated with infancy, the pagan golden age, and the Biblical paradise) to wander through alien lands on a way that rounds imperceptibly back to home and family, but with an accession of insight (the product of her experience en route) which enables her to recognize, in the boy she has left behind, the elusive male figure who has all along been the object of her longing and quest. The protagonist's return home thus coincides with the consummation of a union with her beloved groom.[9]

All typologies are interpretive, a vital point for our typologies of the journey. How far are the patterns of journeying set by the experience of men? In what sense can a woman take a spiritual journey to Italy, to the Eternal City?

Finally, the Italian journey and the *Bildungsreise*. Italy has for centuries been the long-standing goal of an actual educational journey in the sense of a grand tour, a tour that may also become a spiritual journey, like those so well analyzed by M. H. Abrams in his *Natural Supernaturalism*. Italy offers a unique pattern as the goal of a journey. So also does Rome, considered as a metonymy for Italy. Here is one of the centers of classical civilization, and for centuries the center of an *imperium*, an empire. Here, later, for centuries—and still in James's day—remained the sense of a Holy Roman Empire. Here for centuries was the center of Western Christianity, and here still is the center of Western Catholic Christianity. Here is the cradle of the Italian Renaissance. Italy and Rome raise the old great questions. James means his heroine to be seen in that light and against that wide background. He sends her to Rome, a center and a capital and a home already made, for better or for worse.

> It was a matter of course . . . that they should live for the present in Italy. It was in Italy that they had met, Italy had been a party to their first impressions of each other, and Italy should be a party to their happiness. Osmond had the attachment of old acquaintance and Isabel the stimulus of new, which seemed to assure her a future at a high level of consciousness of the beautiful. (p. 297)

James leads his heroine toward the question that lies at the center of his own art, the possible tension between the beautiful and the good, between aesthetics and ethics. He makes of her an example of what it is to be truly civilized. She is in part James himself.

The motif of the journey *in* Italian literature is not complete unless we include the journey *to* Italy in all Western literature.

GIACOMO LEOPARDI: JOURNEY FROM ILLUSIONS TO TRUTH

G. Singh

Illusions—or what he considered to be such—were to play as important a part in Giacomo Leopardi's childhood and early life as in that of any other person. The crucial difference between him and any other person, however, was the extraordinarily swift and unimpeded transition from illusions, however agreeable and even necessary, to truth, however bitter. His journey from the one to the other could not have been briefer or more decisive. "I fanciulli trovano il tutto nel nulla, gli uomini il nulla nel tutto" [children find everything in nothing, men nothing in everything], he was to say in *Zibaldone*.[1] But his own journey from a child's position—seeing "il tutto nel nulla"—to an adult's, seeing "il nulla nel tutto," cannot be measured in terms of time; only in terms of a tacit change within himself that amounted to a sort of moral, psychological, and emotional revolution. From 1809 (when he took his first communion and when, according to his father, he was "sommamente inclinato alla divozione" [greatly inclined to devotion] and "voleva sempre ascoltare molte messe, e chiamava felice quel giorno in cui aveva potuto udirne di piú [always wanted to hear many masses, and called a happy day the day he was able to hear the most])[2] until 1821 (when he composed "Bruto minore," which if not the first is certainly the most explicit and unequivocal statement of his moral and philosophical position), the distance may only have been twelve years; but how many invisible milestones

Leopardi had passed in his inner journey and how many unrecorded incidents in the development of his soul there had been.

Again, while outlining his poetic development in a note he wrote down in *Zibaldone* in 1820, Leopardi was in a way indicating the various stages of his psychological, philosophical, and emotional journey. "Nella carriera poetica," he tells us, echoing both Vico's thought and terminology, "il mio spirito ha percorso lo stesso stadio che lo spirito umano in generale" [in my poetic career, my spirit has gone through the same stage as the human spirit in general]; that is, from imagination to philosophy when, in 1819,

> cominciai a sentire la mia infelicità in un modo assai piú tenebroso ... a riflettere profondamente sopra le cose ... a divenir filosofo di professione (di poeta ch'io era), a sentire l'infelicità certa del mondo, in luogo di conoscerla.
>
> [I started to feel my unhappiness in a much more somber manner ... to reflect profoundly on things ... to become a philosopher by profession (from the poet that I was), to feel the certain unhappiness of the world, instead of knowing it.][3]

This change brought him face-to-face with the goal his mind had been slowly but irresistibly moving toward—the conviction about the "infinita vanità del vero" [the infinite vanity of truth].[4] Yet the vanity of truth did not contradict what was tragically certain about it. Thus, he describes the truth about human destiny, as he saw it, in inflexibly tragic accents in "Bruto minore":

> A voi, marmorei numi
> . . . .
> ... a voi ludibrio e schermo
> È la prole infelice ...
> . . . .
> Guerra mortale, eterna, o fato indegno,

Teco il prode guerreggia,
Di cedere inesperto ...
      In peggio
Precipitano i tempi ...

[To you, oh marble gods
. . . .
... mere sport and mockery
Is that unhappy progeny ...
. . . .
Mortal war, eternal, oh vile fate
With you the brave wages,
Untutored in surrender ...
      To the worse
Our times precipitate ...]

These accents characterize the desperation of one who has come to his journey's end, having traveled a long way during the span of a mere dozen years.

From now on, Leopardi's journey toward truth would continue to be uninterrupted; his thirst for it insatiable, for all its "infinita vanità"; and his passion for it unmatched except by his passion for love. But once he had discovered "l'infinita vanità del tutto" [the infinite vanity of everything] he was left with nothing else to discover. His only task was to come to grips with his experiences, his hopes, disappointments, and disillusions, using truth as the sole criterion, the only point of reference. In other words, if the discovery of truth became the goal of his disillusioned life, the journey toward that goal could never come to an end, because truth or the application of truth could never be exhausted. And even though his mortal journey was coming to an end and he considered himself to be "un sepolcro ambulante, che porta dentro di me un uomo morto" [a walking sepulcher, carrying a corpse within me][5] his consuming passion for truth knew no abating. For having reached his destination once—the discovery of truth—Leopardi resumed his journey again and again to reach the same goal, to discover the same truth.

In fact, if one were to single out one characteristic that, more than any other, distinguishes Leopardi from any other Italian poet (Dante included) and links him with an altogether different cultural and poetic tradition (namely, the English) it would unquestionably be his passion for truth and the untrammeled freedom of thought and independence of mind with which he pursued it. Leopardi's fortune in Victorian as well as in twentieth-century England—and in terms of the weight and variety of critical thought devoted to him, as well as of the competence and distinction of the numerous translations undertaken of his work, it is unparalleled—owed not a little to the recognition and appreciation of this aspect of his poetry, with which readers of Chaucer, Shakespeare, Donne, and Milton, Wordsworth, and T. S. Eliot were so familiar. Bertrand Russell, the most eminent English philosopher and thinker of this century, enjoyed Leopardi's poetry and had this to say in 1967 in a letter to me: "I consider the poetry and pessimism of Leopardi to be the most beautiful expression of what ought to be the creed of a scientist"; and as to "La ginestra," Russell observed that it expresses "more effectively than any other poem known to me my views about the universe and human passions."

It is not that Leopardi followed or cultivated truth, or a particular kind of truth, as one cultivates a particular creed, doctrine, or ideology. Nor did he father or enunciate any particular philosophy. Pessimism is as old as the hills, and its treatment in poetry is found in all ages and climes. Leopardi was not, nor did he profess to be, a philosopher. But what he offers in his poetry and, in a different form in *Operette morali*, is something more than philosophy: it is a fusion, not a dichotomy as Milton saw it, between calm of mind and passion at its most burning. So that what he desires on a sentimental plane—"lingua mortal non dice / quel ch'io sentiva in seno" [Mortal tongue cannot utter / what I felt in my bosom][6]—does not make him less eager on the rational and intellectual plane about the other and equally dominant passion—the passion for truth that is so vital an ingredient of his thought and poetry.

However, Leopardi for all his power of analytical thought—and it was as considerable as that of Coleridge—did not bring any abstract or metaphysical concepts or criteria to bear upon his attitude to or notion of truth. He identified truth, generally speaking, with nature and the reality of things as they are—or as they are seen to be by a mature, disinterested, and disillusioned mind—and with the feelings and sentiments as well as with the thoughts such a view entails. In this respect his attitude to truth is poles apart from that of Keats or Wordsworth. "What the imagination seizes as beauty," says Keats, "must be the truth—whether it existed before or not."[7] And for Wordsworth, the child is the "best philosopher"—"Mighty prophet! Seer blest!? / On whom those truths do rest, / Which we are toiling all our lives to find."[8] But neither what the imagination seizes as beauty nor what the child, "haunted for ever by the eternal mind,"[9] sees was enough for Leopardi's profoundly cultured and skeptical mind. And he could have said to both the Wordsworthian child and to Keats, what he says in a vein of poetic irony to the moon in "Canto notturno":

> Ma tu per certo,
> Giovinetta immortal, conosci il tutto,
> Questo io conosco e sento,
> Che degli eterni giri,
> Che dell'esser mio frale,
> Qualche bene o contento
> Avrà fors'altri; a me la vita è male.

> [But you, for certain,
> Immortal maiden, know all,
> This I know and feel,
> That in eternal cycles,
> That in my frail being,
> Some good, some happiness,
> Others perhaps can find; life to me is evil.]

It is, therefore, not what his imagination seizes, but what he knows and what he perceives to be the real truth—the processes of "knowing" and "feeling" being inseparable in Leopardi's perception of truth—that ultimately counts, for one who was free from illusions and who at the same time celebrated eloquently their value and efficacy in human life. But however strongly he might have felt the spell of illusions or envied those who find "qualche bene o contento" in the "eterni giri," it never distracted him from his unswerving quest for truth, his moral integrity, and his belief that "a me la vita è male." The silence of the stars frightened Pascal; the "interminati spazi" [interminable spaces] "sovrumani silenzi" [superhuman silences] and "profondissima quiete" [deepest silence] almost frightened Leopardi and dramatically heightened his sense of the contrast between the finiteness of his "esser mio frale" and the infinity of the universe, which made him cling all the more passionately and determinedly to his own convictions. Leopardi's passion for truth, as he saw it (even though it was inimical to happiness), became for him a matter of personal honor, pride, and integrity; it was not merely a philosophical pursuit but also a moral concern. In all of Leopardi's poetry we find accents of personal moral pride as a result of his total commitment to truth—accents that add a peculiar potency to his lyricism, for which one looks in vain in the works of his contemporaries. In the poetry of Wordsworth, another votary of truth, what we have is something quite different. In Wordsworth's best poetry, as in Leopardi's, moral fervor and poetic fervor almost always go together. But unlike Leopardi, whose gaze remained fixed uncompromisingly on the truths of life really lived, Wordsworth habitually shifted his gaze from the outer to the inner, from the visible to the visionary, from earth to heaven. Not only that, but he sees truth as being in the nature of (to quote his own words) something half-perceived and half-created. It was, in the last analysis, a product of his own mind or, as Leopardi says of love, "la figlia / Della sua mente" [the daughter of his mind].[10] Hence, with regard to the kind of truths that nourished Wordsworth's poetic life, one might say (as Coleridge did) about the various aspects of nature: "O Lady! we receive but what we give, / And in our life alone does Nature live."[11]

But the kind of truth that interested Leopardi, which he celebrated in his poetry and which constitutes its moral and philosophical backbone, is a truth that originates from firsthand experience or from an unbiased and disinterested observation of nature and society. It is not something half-perceived and half-created. The poet has no choice but to present what he sees around him, what he feels within himself, and what his insatiably exploratory and analytical mind presents him with or forces upon him. If Wordsworth was a seer in the idealistic sense and Blake in the visionary sense, Leopardi was a seer in the most rational and realistic sense of the term.

In fact, Wordsworth thought he derived his light from heaven and that he shone to the measure of that heaven-born light, rather than to the measure of the light born out of his everyday experiences and observations. That is why his truths no less than his sense of reality have an essentially idealistic rather than empirical basis, even though he chose to deal with "incidents and situations from common life" and to write about them in "a selection of language really used by men."[12] For Leopardi, on the contrary, the source of inspiration was nothing more than his own thoughts, experiences, and observations concerning life; and there was no consolation for him except in truth, however bitter and unconsolatory it might have been. Leopardi considered truth to be neither beautiful nor conducive to happiness. The knowledge of truth, he tells us, "non sarà mai sorgente di felicità, né oggi; né era allora quando uomo primitivo se la passava nella solitudine, ben lontano certamente dalle meditazioni filosofiche" [will never spring from happiness, neither today, nor did it before when primitive man spent his time in solitude, clearly a long way from philosophical meditations].[13] Nevertheless, so far as he was concerned, however unpalatable or unflattering the truth he pursued it unflinchingly and made it known in his writings, even at the risk of incurring oblivion in his own age or in posterity ("obblio / Preme chi troppo all'età propria increbbe" [oblivion / weighs heavy on he who displeases his own times][14] by telling people what they do not want to know but what a man like him, once he has seen it or known it himself, cannot forbear from telling; any more than he can unsee it or unknow it. Leopardi's English counterpart, Thomas Hardy, after decades of writing and unbaring what people did not want to know promised himself, toward the end of his life that he would not anymore reveal what he saw. In his poem "He Resolves to Say No More," published posthumously and presumably written in the last year of his life, he tells himself (more or less in the same philosophically disillusioned vein as Leopardi in "A se stesso"):

> O my soul keep the rest unknown!
> It is too like a sound of moan . . .
> Why load men's minds with more to bear
> That bear already ails to spare?
>   From now alway
>   Till my last day
> What I discern I will not say.[15]

But, for one thing, Leopardi was too young and too passionately interested in the discovery, analysis, and exposition of what he considered to be real to want to or to be able to afford to make such a resolution; for another, his need to attest to the truth and reality of what most people ignore (or prefer to ignore because it is not conducive to their happiness) was too great a necessity of his own soul and being to be set aside. It was something he could live by, and he assumed that spirits congenial to his own could also live by it. I am thinking of the Scottish poet Edwin Muir, who called Leopardi and Baudelaire Romantic, in the bad sense, because for him they merely portrayed the sufferings of existence and merely questioned fate. They expressed an attitude to life, he tells us, "a perfectly genuine one too—but not a principle of life, not something by which one can live."[16] Leopardi would have retorted that for most people the principle they live by is to avoid, as far as possible, facing the unpleasant truths forced upon them in the course of living.

He compared humankind's attitude in general to unpalatable truths, to husbands' attitudes to wives: "I mariti, se vogliono viver tranquilli, è necessario che credano le moglie fedeli, ciascuno la sua; e così fanno; anche quando la metà del mondo sa che il vero è tutt'altro" [Married men, if they want to live in peace, must believe their wives to be faithful, each man his own; and that's what they do; even when half the world knows the truth is totally different]. And this because "il genere umano crede sempre, non il vero, ma quello che è, o pare che sia, più a proposito suo" [human beings believe, not the truth, but what is, or seems to be, more convenient to them].[17] For Leopardi such pragmatism was utterly out of place and inconceivable, and he could well have said, with Dante, that what he has seen and known, "mentr'io vivo / Convien che nella mia lingua si scerna" [while I live / it is possible to see this in my life and in my art][18]—which is precisely what he did and continued doing until the very end of his life. To camouflage or suppress the bitter truths of life was too ignominious and cowardly for him: "Non io / Con tal vergogna scenderò sotterra" [not I, not with that shame shall I die], he tells us in "La ginestra." It was not so much pride in a personal sense as pride on account of his espousing truth at the expense of personal comfort and happiness that mattered to him both as a poet and as a man. Such pride contributed to the tone and timber of his verse as much as did his supreme mastery over style and diction. It also enabled him to accept the common lot of a man, "nato a perir, nutrito in pene" [born to perish, reared in pain], as the subject matter of his poetry rather than the glorification of "eccelsi fati e nove / Felicità, quali il ciel tutto ignora. / Non pur quest'orbe" [sublime destinies and new / Happiness, of a kind that Heaven ignores / not the least of which those of this world].[19]

In this respect, therefore, Leopardi could have turned to Wordsworth, or rather to his spokesman and admirer Matthew Arnold, and said that the joy offered to us in nature that, according to Arnold, constitutes Wordsworth's supremacy over Leopardi, may be "accessible universally," but it needs a particularly gifted nature like Wordsworth's to be able to profit from it. Thus, it can hardly be said to form a part of the "comun fato" [common destiny] that was the "haunt, and the main region" of Leopardi's song.[20] In depicting the lot of common mortals, Leopardi chose the image of the "vecchierel bianco, infermo. / Mezzo vestito e scalzo, / Con gravissimo fascio sulle spalle" [white-haired wise old man, infirm / Barely clad and bare footed / A heavy burden on his shoulders], and not that of one belonging to "a privileged world / Within a world," such as Shakespeare or Milton whom Wordsworth calls "labourers divine!"[21] It is true that the leech-gatherer, protagonist of Wordsworth's great poem "Resolution and Independence," may be regarded as being in some ways a Wordsworthian counterpart, if not equivalent, of Leopardi's "vecchierel bianco, infermo." But although the Leopardian model symbolizes a condition of existence that is all too common, almost universal, the Wordsworthian model embodies qualities one aspires to, or ought to aspire to, but seldom attains. Thus the leech-gatherer is more of an ideal than a symbol of, to quote Wordsworth's own words, "what is to be borne"—and borne by all and sundry without exception.

Hence the ethos as well as the essence of Leopardi's thought and sentiment—and in Leopardi the two are seldom apart—derive from his concern with what is true of human nature and human destiny in general rather than from his interest in what befalls the lot of only some exceptionally gifted and privileged individuals and their not less privileged experiences. Take, for instance, such lines as

> Io sono distrutto
> Né schermo alcun ho dal dolore,
> . . . .
> Amore,
> Amor, di nostra vita ultimo inganno

[I am destroyed
No shield whatever have I from pain,
. . . .
Love,
Love, of our life the ultimate deception][22]

... non le tinte glebe,
Non gli ululati spechi
Turbò nostra sciagura,
Né scolorò le stelle umana cura

[... neither the bloodstained lands,
Nor the echoing caves
have been troubled by our misfortune,
Nor have human cares dimmed the stars][23]

Oh come grato occorre
Nel tempo giovanil, quando ancor lungo
La speme e breve ha la memoria il corso,
Il rimembrar delle passate cose,
Ancor che triste, e che l'affanno duri!

[Oh how pleasant it is
In time of youth, when hope is still
Long and the span of memory short,
To remember things past,
Though be they sad, and though the anguish endures!][24]

... perché giacendo
A bell'agio, ozioso,
S'appaga ogni animale;
Me, s'io giaccio in riposo, il tedio assale?

[... why is
Every animal content
Lying idle at perfect ease;
Why, if I lie down to rest, does boredom seize me?][25]

Uscir di pena
È diletto fra noi,

[To overcome hardship
Is for us delight][26]

Misterio eterno
Dell'esser nostro

[Eternal mystery
Of our being][27]

Ma la vita mortal, poi che la bella
Giovinezza sparí, non si colora
D'altra luce giammai, né d'altra aurora.

[But mortal life, once fair
Youth has vanished, never takes on the colors
Of another light, nor of another dawn.][28]

Magnanimo animale
Non credo io già, ma stolto,
Quel che nato a perir, nutrito in pene,
Dice, a goder son fatto.

[I do not, at all believe him
A noble-minded creature who,
Born to perish, reared in pain,
Claims, I was made to find enjoyment.][29]

In such lines, Leopardi's thought and sentiment have all the marks of an intensely personal participation in what he is talking about. But what he is talking about concerns not his own self or situation, but that of mankind in general. And if he generalizes on the basis of his own experience, as one often does, his generalizations are not the less valid for that. The language of these generalizations bears the mark of Leopardi's genius; but the moral as well as the logical cogency behind them confers upon them a universal character, not because he transforms something that has merely a personal validity or relevance into something universally valid, but because—such is his burning passion for truth—he cannot contemplate what has a universal application without identifying himself with it at a personal level. As the "sounding cataract" haunted the young Wordsworth, reflections about human destiny—the nature of what is real and what is to be borne as distinguished from what is illusory and fragile in human life, hopes, and aspirations—haunted Leopardi "like a passion";[30] that is why his thoughts are expressed not so much in philosophical terms, as in poetically charged ones. No philosopher, said Leopardi, can do without a system, but he himself had none. What he did have were those qualities he considered indispensable to a philosopher:

> Chi non ha o non ha mai avuto . . . immaginazione, sentimento, capacità di entusiasmo, di eroismo, d'illusioni vive e grandi, di forti e varie passioni, chi non conosce l'immenso sistema del bello, chi non legge o non sente, o non ha mai letto o sentito i poeti, non può assolutamente essere un grande, vero e perfetto filosofo, anzi non sarà mai se non un filosofo dimezzato, di corta vista, di colpo d'occhio assai debole, di penetrazione scarsa, per diligente, paziente, e sottile, e dialettico e matematico ch'ei possa essere; non conoscerà mai il vero, si persuaderà e proverà colla possibile evidenza cose falsissime.

> [He who does not have or has never had . . . imagination, feeling, capacity for enthusiasm, for heroism, for grand and ardent illusions, for strong and varied passions, who does not know the vast system of beauty, who does not read or does not feel, or who has never read the poets or listened to them, can certainly never be a great true, or perfect philosopher. In fact, he will never be anything but a cloven philosopher, short-sighted, with dull glance, and feeble insight, however diligent, patient, subtle, dialectical, and mathematical he may be; he will never know the truth, and he will come to believe and prove, as true things that are utterly false.][31]

Leopardi's passion for truth was, therefore, the passion of a philosopher as well as that of a poet. But it was above all the passion of one who found the ultimate confirmation of what he thought in his own experience, observation, and thought, rather than in any theory, dogma, or philosophy.

And although the more he pursued truth the more he found it inimical to happiness, this did not prevent him from carrying on the pursuit intrepidly; nor did it prevent him from celebrating the beauty, sweetness, and soothing power of illusions, because he realized the essential emptiness of life without them (and, in the case of one like himself with his unstinting acceptance of "l'acerbo vero" [the bitter truth] even with them).[32] The contrast between what is true and what is illusory, between what people choose to believe because it is comfortable and conducive to their happiness—as summed up by Browning in "God's in His Heaven, / All's right with the world!"[33]—and what the facts of life in reality are or what they appear to be to an insatiably searching and relentlessly honest mind is the predominant theme in Leopardi's writings, the focal point to which all his moral as well as philosophical reflections and excogitations converge. That is why Leopardi's convictions have the air of incontrovertible certitude about them, which goes a long way toward explaining the masterly simplicity, poise, and perfection of his style. Truth creates its own style, said Ezra Pound, whose translation of Leopardi's "Sopra il ritratto di una bella donna" stands out among all the English and American translations of Leopardi's *Canti*. Hence truth and Leopardi's attitude to it determine his style as much as his extraordinary powers of expression and technique.

One of the most conspicuous features of his style and mode of expression is the exceptional degree of calm and even detachment behind them, even when he is dealing with the strongest passions and emotions. It is for this reason that some English critics of Leopardi in the nineteenth century—Charles Edwardes and H. F. Brown, for instance—compared him with Sakyamuni (the Buddha). Seekers of truth, Buddha thought, cannot attain enlightenment unless their passions are calmed. There is, one might say, a dispassionateness in Leopardi's poetry, which is a reflection or consequence of his implicit acceptance of truth, however detrimental that might be to his own peace or happiness. Even in his protestations against nature—

> O natura, natura
> Perché non rendi poi
> Quel che prometti allor?
>
> [Oh nature, nature
> Why do you not yield afterward
> What you promised then?][34]

—there is an element of stoic calm and dispassionateness that Leopardi associated with the "nobil natura," which, like Leopardi himself,

> ... a sollevar s'ardisce
> Gli occhi mortali incontra
> Al comun fato, e che con franca lingua,
> Nulla al ver detraendo,
> Confessa il mal che ci fu dato in sorte.
>
> [... that ventures to look up
> Through mortal eyes to meet
> Our common fate, and with truthful tongue,
> Nothing subtracting from the truth,
> Admits the evil lot assigned to us as destiny][35]

How many resources of strength this sickly and unhappy poet had at his command can be gauged from his unswerving devotion to and single-minded passion for truth, and from the calm grandeur and crystalline clarity of his style. Each of Leopardi's *Canti* manifests these qualities, but none so superbly as "Canto notturno di un pastore errante dell'Asia," where the silence of the moon may be compared with Buddha's in the face of the unanswerable questions the shepherd—and Leopardi's mouthpiece—confronts it with:

> ... a che vale
> Al pastor la sua vita,

> La vostra vita a voi? . . . ove tende
> Questo vagar mio breve,
> Il tuo corso immortale?
> . . . .
> Se la vita è sventura,
>
> Perché da noi si dura?
> . . . .
> Che fa l'aria infinita, e quel profondo
> Infinito seren?
>
> [. . . what is his life worth
> To the shepherd,
> Or your life to you? . . . where does it lead
> This brief wandering of mine,
> And your immortal course,
> . . . .
> If life is misfortune,
>
> Why do we endure?
> . . . .
> What makes the skies infinite, and that infinite
> Space serene?][36]

It is of the very essence of Leopardi's integrity as a seeker after truth that he not only asks these questions but also refrains from giving implausible, still less insincere answers to them. Hence the ironical drift of his supposition that what he does not know and therefore cannot answer, the moon, being immortal, might know. But in directing the irony against the moon Leopardi is in fact directing it against himself—insofar as he knows full well that the questions he is asking the moon are by their very nature unanswerable. The silence of the moon cannot be interpreted, as Buddha's silence has sometimes been, as an expression of suspended judgment; for Leopardi it is, as it were, the dumb answering the dumb, and if no answer is given, it is because there is none to give.

Leopardi's passion for truth brought him face-to-face with the unfathomable mystery of life, with the unanswerable questions concerning the universe and human destiny, and he realized, quite early on in life, that the universe is indifferent to man's ethical striving—

> Non ha natura al seme
> Dell'uom piú stima o cura
> Che alla formica.
>
> [Nature has no more regard or care
> For the seed of man
> Than she does for an ant.][37]

But his view of life "in questo oscuro / Granel di sabbia" [in this obscure grain of sand][38] remained full of its moral content, that is, the values and criteria governing human conduct. Leopardi may not have said with Matthew Arnold that three-fourths of life is conduct, but he would have agreed with him that poetry, and indeed all literature, is at bottom a criticism of life, as his own writings so convincingly demonstrate. Considering man to be "in tutto il nostro globo la cosa piú nobile" [in our entire world the most noble thing],[39] "la principale opera della natura terrestre, o sia del nostro pianeta" [the most important work of earthly nature, that is, of our planet], Leopardi could not but interpret his position both vis-à-vis other men and the "brutto poter . . . ascoso" [brutal power . . . secret] of the universe in broadly moral terms.[40] The very connection between life with illusions and life without them, between illusion and reality, between "uom di povero stato e membra inferme" [man in poor and sickly condition] and "nobil natura" [noble nature], is by its very nature of a profoundly moral order.[41] And "l'acerbo, indegno mistero delle cose" [the bitter, unkind mystery of things],[42] with which Leopardi's passion for truth had to reckon, served only to strengthen his sense of the categorical imperatives of a moral and social life and make his need to embody them in his own daily life all the greater, even though (to quote Omar Khayyám) "tomorrow I may be / Myself with yesterday's Sev'n Thousand Years."[43]

OF SWALLOWS AND FAREWELLS: THE MORALITY OF MOVEMENT IN ITALIAN LITERATURE OF THE *OTTOCENTO*

Antonino Musumeci

> Da te lontano empio destin mi mena
> e mi divide per sempre da te.
> Andrò ramingo in qualche ignota arena,
> le tue memorie portando con me.
> Lunge da te sgradita
> mi sembrerà la vita.
>
> [Away from you wicked destiny takes me
> and separates me from you forever.
> I shall go wandering in some unknown arena,
> carrying with me memories of you.
> Away from you, to me
> life will seem unpleasant.]
>
> G. Giusti, "Addio"

From Ulysses to Pascal, to the *déraciné* of neopicaresque fiction, motion seems to have always been charged with value. A simple voyage can become an ascension, a descent, a quest, or a pilgrimage, and can extend its wanderings into the comforting regions of memory or the uncharted landscape of the subconscious. It is through journeying that the heros and heroines of many tales and a thousand faces fulfill their mythical potential and attain true knowledge.[1] The history of a nation has been defined by its movement westward, as if answering the irresistible pull of a powerful magnet suggesting a master plan in the events of the human race. Even science, in its hours of imagination, dreams of voyages into yet unknown spaces—inner or outer, micro or cosmic—and, if the Star Wars saga portends epiphanies of things to come, the destiny of the human race will be an endless journey through the expanding vastness of the universe, engaged in the ultimate struggle of Good versus Evil. Indeed, life itself has found in that metaphor a connatural referential term, and death its final image.

The story of the human race glistens with tales of great voyages: Adam and Eve's expulsion from the land of permanence and grace into the world of sinfulness, pain, and temporality; Jason's daring sea voyage on the Quest of the Golden Fleece (the prototype for a hundred similar adventures in the course of time—Columbus and the Indies, Magellan and the passage to the West, Livingstone and Victoria Falls); the Wright brothers' gliding away from the force that had always denied verticality; Sputnik's alluring venture toward that new space that Daedalus had long ago suggested, and so on.

But the greatest voyages have been those of the mind, and poets and mystics the greatest adventurers. Journeys are the stuff folktales and myths are made of, and much literature as well. Whereas crusaders and merchants, explorers and scholars, *clerici vagantes* [wandering clerics] and missionaries did indeed sail to unfamiliar geographies—attaining thereby in the popular imagination the exotic (and therefore abnormal) quality and the otherness of the faraway lands they had visited—the space open to everyone's exploration was the one charted by the mind, and the pioneers in that space were Homer and Ulysses, Virgil and Aeneas, Moses and the People of the Exodus, Alighieri and the wayfaring Dante, Swift and Gulliver. To most, the journey was above all a metaphor, an adventure in the spiritual, aesthetic, or existential dimension, in nonspatial coordinates. Perhaps for that reason movement has become such a powerful allegory, has been endowed with meaning beyond its purely locomotive ambulatory connotation, and has been elevated to a moral category.[2]

F. Hayez. *I vespri siciliani* (Sicilian Vespers). 1846. Oil on canvas, 225 x 300 cm. Galleria Nazionale d'Arte Moderna, Rome.

But with the cosmopolitanism of the Enlightenment of the late *Settecento*, with the existential need of the Romanticism of the early *Ottocento* to find in a particular geography the analogue of its inner state (if not the hope for a therapy for its restlessness), and above all with the economic possibilities and the necessities peculiar to the bourgeoisie (which was rapidly becoming at that time the dominant social class in Europe), spatial travel begins to be a reality, not just in flights of fancy but in measurable physical distances. The Grand Tour, no longer an aristocratic prerogative, extends its call to a new generation of eager travelers, promising pleasure, novelty, adventure, discovery of old cultures and new markets, enrichment of the mind and of the purse. The travel agent cannot be far behind and, beaconed by the hissing melody of the steam engine (like the magical sound of a mechanical Piper of Hamelin), leisure travel becomes an industry.[3]

Italian society, too, in the *Ottocento*—though late with respect to some northern European nations, and burdened by its ancient endemic problems and by the no longer postponable project of national unification—slowly evolves toward the establishment of a middle class. In fact, the process of *imborghesimento* [bourgeoisification] of the peninsula runs parallel, and at one point becomes identical, with that of the Risorgimento. For the tortuous itinerary of national unification, the bourgeoisie emerged with an enormous new certainty: that the destiny of the country was to be identifiable and coextensive with its own class interests—the "Nuova Italia" would be necessarily bourgeois, and its future necessarily industrial and capitalistic.

Within this framework, I ask, what was the prevailing attitude toward movement in Italy in the *Ottocento*? And in my search for an answer I leaf through the literary works of that age, works that are rapidly coming to reflect the values of the middle class. And the answer, I believe, is overwhelmingly uniform. Physical mobility in space is a negative and dangerous experience; it is a moving away from a valued condition, not a moving toward a promising potentiality (as such it cannot be enriching but must be depriving, for it causes absences and pain); it can be imposed by powerful diabolical forces or inevitable historical necessities, but in either case it should be resisted if possible and rapidly terminated, to reestablish the original state of stasis in familiar confines. The concept of mobility is branded with a negative moral connotation; the only positive movement is the one that takes place in the realms of the mind or the spirit, still a metaphor, still a dream.

In Manzoni's *I promessi sposi*, mobility is not chosen or welcome but is rather the result of the disruptive intrusion of socially unjust and morally corrupt powers into the lives of the protagonists. The legitimate desire for fulfillment in the static accepted normalcy of the community, which marriage would consecrate and ensure, is subverted, giving rise to suffering, distance, abnormal experiences, bodily and spiritual dangers. Renzo's and Lucia's are not purposeful journeys but escapes; they do not lead to any goal or destination; above all, they do not allow for a return. Even after the evil forces that prompted that mobility are rendered ineffectual, the condition associated with the original stasis can no longer be salvaged. Once the otherness of space has been experienced, the idyllic state is lost forever, and even God's corrective intervention into the history of humankind apparently cannot restore it. Mobility has made them different. As Adam's children they can attain heaven but not the Garden of Eden; after the experience of evil, they can achieve sainthood but they cannot regain innocence. So they will settle somewhere else, away from the space that was originally destined to be theirs, in limbo, in exile.[4] In that new dimension of happiness regained (but no longer of innocence), Renzo draws a double conclusion from his adventures. The one shared with Lucia is spiritual in nature, alludes to a better world, and restates in simple theological terms the Christian perception of the problem of evil ["i guai"];[5] the other is Renzo's very own, pragmatic in nature, rooted in the real world, a proclamation of complete disengagement from the social context and the renunciation of mobility as capable of producing positive experiences.[6] If (as has been stated) *I promessi sposi* is the novel of the bourgeoisie, describing some of its uncertainties, then among the assertions of bourgeois values and the revelations of its phobias, we notice the condemnation of mobility as unredemptive and disruptive.

In the world of Foscolo even happiness is denied. If, for many Romantics (especially the English), exile was a chosen condition, not so for Foscolo: he believed he was born under that dispensation and that Zacynthos, as the unattainable island of his birth, was the mythical prefiguration of a destiny, the anticipation of his existence, a prophecy "sempre fuggendo / di gente in gente" [forever fleeing from country to country].[7] Since the poet is born under the sign those who are "senza patria" [without a homeland], Fate has decreed for him endless mobility, to reflect his inner restlessness. And he paints a gallery of self-images, from Ortis to Homer, all exiles, all without a homeland, wanderers heroic in their roles, chasing an ever elusive tranquillity or rummaging through cultural wastelands. Exile (as Ovid feared) is above all a threat to one's cultural memory and therefore to one's very identity.[8] Foscolo, unlike Manzoni, does not possess the certainty of a gratuitous promise of happiness; but he does have the boundless Romantic faith in poetic discourse. And so he makes poetry his exile, and his muse of the resultant despair. Poetry, in its powerful fragility, is for Foscolo the only antidote to the mobility imposed by Fate. It is culture that can give stability and continuity to the precariousness of history, and poetry that can make of history not only a memory but also a prophetic expectation.[9]

For a time, at least, Leopardi wished for Foscolo's fate; but in short order he abandoned the adolescent hope that his anguish could be cured or at least alleviated by distancing himself from the provincial strictures of Recanati and the suffocating tentacles of his family. In the *Operette morali* the meditation on the potential value of mobility—as an attempt at dealing with the problem of human suffering—is constant and protracted, and it always concludes with the denial of any salvific resolution from such a strategy. In the "Dialogo della Natura e di un Islandese" the protagonist, threatened by social intercourse and ontologically insecure, travels through most of the world in an effort to escape the defining characteristics of human nature—"mi posi a cangiar luoghi e climi, per vedere se in alcuna parte della terra potessi non offendendo non essere offeso, e non godendo non patire" [I resolved to change place and clime, to see if there was any part of the world where I might, without offending anyone or being offended, if not be happy, at least not suffer]—only to find that the gigantic female figure he has been talking to, in the last stretches of uninhabited territory, is Nature herself. Mobility has brought no relief; at the end of the journey there is no haven. The only contribution journeying can make in the existential struggle is to create short-lived illusions ("per un tempo . . . ci tiene liberi dalla noia, ci fa cara la vita" [for a time . . . keeps us free from boredom and makes our lives very dear]),[10] only to realize soon enough that "vita e infelicità non si possono scompagnare" [life and unhappiness are inseparable companions][11] and that "il male è cosa comune a tutti i pianeti dell'universo" [evil is common to all the planets of the universe][12] and "ogni parte dell'universo si affretta infaticabilmente alla morte, con sollecitudine e celerità mirabile" [every part of the universe hurries untiringly toward death with haste and amazing speed].[13] Leopardi's reflection is too earnest in its cogency, too relentless in its stringency, not to disavow the Romantic faith in traveling as an evasion from the existential prison or the facile bourgeois ritual of a therapeutic vacation.

This is not to say that Italians did not travel during the *Ottocento*, even beyond the pseudo-journey between "casa di città" [city dwelling] and "casa di campagna" [country house]—some Italians even went away to war. An analysis of the so-called patriotic poetry of the period will reveal, I believe, as the dominant theme of these compositions not the euphoria of the adventurous projection into a space to be saved and reclaimed under the tricolor in fulfillment of a general longing, but rather the sense of perilousness caused by the departure, the fear for severed relationships, the anxious waiting to return to the ancestral grounds. This is poetry born of the people, closer in form and sentiment to dialectal expressions than to the models of a consecrated literary tradition; and as such it proclaims values of a circumscribed place, and within that space, values and icons of the home: "la sposa, il genitore, i figli, la ragazza, il focolare, il campo, il fazzoletto, la ciocca di capelli" [the bride, the parent, the children, the girl, the hearth, the field, the handkerchief, the lock of hair], and so on. It is also a poetry of heroes; but in the shadow of the obvious mythical figures—(Garibaldi, Mazzini, "il volontario," "la garibaldina" [the volunteer, the Garibaldina])—moves an anonymous host of equally heroic characters—"il profugo," "il fuoruscito," "l'esiliato," "il pellegrino," "il coscritto," "il reduce" [the refugee, the émigré, the exile, the pilgrim, the conscript, the veteran]—faceless images of reluctant travelers, apt to solicit immediate identification and projections of a thousand individual stories evolving into legends. This expression of the experience of the Risorgimento finds its complement in the writings of those who reflected upon it. Whether political in scope, or documentary moving toward the epic, such memorialist literature lacks in general the simplicity and the immediacy of patriotic poetry.[14] But these examples of memorialist literature represent acts of witnessing that become verbal testimonies precisely because the element of anxiety of the actual event of the past and its attendant mobility have now been resolved into the comforting confines of the home now safely regained, and from that privileged space, the mind that remembers fondly lingers over the "other" places and the unique experiences and proudly asserts: "I was there! I saw it!" It is immobility that allows for the pleasurable recollection of mobility, now tamed and exorcised.

Closer in character to patriotic poetry are the works of those poets unfortunately labeled as minor. In reality, the very magnitude of their production and its mediocre quality represent perhaps a more accurate reading of the cultural pulse of a people. A consideration of their works would bring us to similar conclusions.[15] First of all, the lexical terms chosen to describe movement fall within the semantic field of suffering: "partenza, fuga, lontananza, addio, commiato, errare, solitudine, lamento" [departure, flight, absence, farewell, leave-taking, wandering, solitude, lament], and so on. Privileged among these is the moment of the "addio," a scene obsessively repeated throughout Italian literature of the nineteenth century, from the highly poetic and eloquent archetype in *I promessi sposi* to the painfully unuttered version in *I Malavoglia*: a scene that suggests at its core an act of looking back at what one is being separated from, not the looking forward to new encounters. And the "rondine" [swallow] is the symbol that is called upon to embody the sentiment of parting and the concomitant hope of its positive resolution in an eventual return: equally ubiquitous, the swallow flies through prose and poetry alike, qualified as "peregrina" [wandering]. In the travel lexicon of this age the only terms that denote a positive experience are "passeggio, passeggiata, scampagnata" [promenade, stroll, country trip] (and very few others), that is, terms that describe non-journeys, or spurts of mobility within a well-defined and familiar space, terms that come with the inbuilt promise of an immediate return, terms that allow for the destination to be the same as the place one has just left. And whenever verbal expressions of movement are used, they are defined by pseudolocative complements ("nella memoria; nell'azzurro; in libreria" [in memory; in the sky; in the bookstore]), and so on, or by a modifier that reduces it to a metaphoric experience ("spirituale; capriccioso") [spiritual; capricious]. The prepositions that typically accompany an expression of movement impart to the journey a vertical, thus metaphoric, direction ("in su; in alto") [upward; up above] rather than indicate actual mobility through space, such as *forward, beyond, from, toward, into, through*, which instead are quite common in English equivalents.[16] Even the form proclaims the desired message.

With the enforcement of the "Legge Casati" (1859)—designed to restructure the school system and make school attendance mandatory—along with the increasing bourgeois concern with education, there arose in Italy in the second half of the *Ottocento* the need, and therefore the availability, of new usage of the written word. In addition to textbooks and books for pleasure (Salgari), there were also works linked to the so-called "letteratura della bontà" [literature of edification], which were directed specifically to children. Unequaled among these were De Amicis's *Cuore* (1886) and Collodi's *Le avventure di Pinocchio* (1883). Their popularity and influence in molding the character of generations of young readers can be surmised in Franco Ferrucci's assertion that "i soli libri dello scorso secolo che siano entrati in tutte le classi sociali sono *I promessi sposi, Pinocchio e Cuore*" [The only books from the last century that have reached all social classes are *I promessi sposi, Pinocchio,* and *Cuore*].[17] They are in fact catechisms of bourgeois values, nurturing virtues and condemning vices that derive their "morality" precisely from those values and revealing at the same time the ethical canons and also the hypocrisies of that social class. Important, apparently, among the temptations to be resisted is the danger of mobility, as Pinocchio's story makes quite evident. Pinocchio's problem is an enormous one: he is suffering under the worst possible case of abnormality. All he wants is to be normal, to become a real boy, with flesh and bones, like any other kid. But his attempts (and we notice that they all imply mobility away from home) all make his predicament worse, until he is in danger of losing even the discursive ability he retained as a wooden puppet and of becoming an animal—until, that is, he accepts the value system of a "bravo bambino" [good boy] and renounces mobility as an effort to find a remedy for his abnormal condition somewhere else (other than in the space of the family within the perimeter of the community). The fulfillment of one's desires cannot be achieved through mobility, but rather through the acceptance of class creeds.

The great editorial *coup de maître* [masterstroke] of the nineteenth century was the feuilleton: a new public, eager to read, found in that form one of its chosen pastimes. And the "romanzi d'appendice" [serial novels] became in short order (and remained well into the twentieth century) the most popular reading of the bourgeoisie, which rewarded its favorite authors (Carolina Invernizio and Guido da Verona) with a financial success until then denied to writers. These novels were aimed at a specific audience (the urban bourgeoisie, especially women); they have a specific function (the immediate gratification of the reader); they are supported by a specific ideology (that of the status quo, which favors the dominant class); and they are constructed in a specific manner.[18] They describe a Manichaen conflict between Good and Evil; the conclusion of the story is already known, and only its resolution remains uncertain. The denouement has to ensure the reconstitution of order, of the family, of the social good according to bourgeois morality. The journey has an ample role in these "romanzi di consumo" [popular novels]; its function is twofold, psychological and ideological: to alleviate the boredom of the reader by tantalizing her with an exotic world radically different from her monotonous daily routine, and to warn her by examples that mobility away from the family and the established role within one's social class can cause only destruction and pain. The mobility of the protagonists of these novels has the function of recommending immobility to the readers.

Verga's great *verista* [realistic] novel *I Malavoglia* also advises against mobility. The conflict that threatens the house by the medlar tree is not merely generational but fundamentally ideological: it is a conflict between the traditionalist on the one hand (padron 'Ntoni) who would consider faithfulness to established values the ultimate goal, and the social climber on the other ('Ntoni) who would abandon those values for economic benefit. Movement in the novel is both real and symbolic, that is, it implies a moving away from a traditional way of life and an aspiring to economic well-being in a social environment that is radically different. But whether real or symbolic, mobility is condemned with equal vigor. All those who move away from Aci Trezza, whatever the reason for their departure, come to a sad end: Lisa is infected by the corruption of urban life; Luca dies in the waters during the Battle of Lissa; even Alfio—who, for the exercise of his profession, needs the limited mobility afforded by his cart—cannot fulfill his desire and is ostracized to the otherness of unfamiliar space. The real mobile character is 'Ntoni, who dreams of finding elsewhere the opportunity for success, and precisely for that reason he becomes responsible for the catastrophe that befalls the family and the house. 'Ntoni's renewed, periodic mobility is seen as corruptive and destructive of the wholeness of the family, and therefore punishable with banishment from the home, a punishment of biblical severity: as Adam is forever cut off from the realm of innocence and grace, so 'Ntoni is forever cast into the darkness of the other space. The novel ends as Rocco Spatu begins his day in the village (marginal though he is to the rhythm of its life) and as 'Ntoni takes his leave from it. The only difference between the two is that 'Ntoni has succumbed to the allure of mobility, and for that reason he is severed from family and community and is cast away.

It is perhaps presumptuous for a literary critic to attempt to diagnose social and cultural phenomena: the closer we analyze the relationship between empirical reality and the literary text approximating it, the larger the distance between the two seems to grow. Perhaps all that literature can do is emit performative utterances.[19] But curiosity does persist; and to attempt to appease that curiosity, I will advance some possible reasons for the condemnatory attitude toward mobility that seems to pervade Italian literature of the *Ottocento*. There are cultural reasons that arbitrarily codify a certain behavior and eventually attach to it a patina of acceptability, if not morality. In the case that concerns us here, I find in an early poem by Pavese (a writer who for his own artistic purposes had to violate this negative moral connotation of mobility) a succinct expression of such cultural determination:

> Almeno potercene andare,
> Far la libera fame, rispondere no

> A una vita che adopera amore e pietà,
> La famiglia, il pezzetto di terra, a legarci le mani.
>
> [At least to be able to leave,
> to suffer hunger in freedom, to say no
> to a life that uses love and piety,
> family, a plot of land, to tie us down.][20]

Italy is a country of frontiers not to be transcended but to be respected; its values have been values of permanence, not of projection. To that we could add the elitist attitude of the post-Renaissance Classicist tradition, which dominated intellectual life for centuries and which espoused a policy of cultural elitism: the best that the human mind had to offer had already been served and could be found on the Italian table. It is precisely in the *Ottocento* that such an attitude was finally challenged by the first generation of Italian Romanticists.

But I would like to propose an additional reason, suggested by the work of Michel Foucault. With the advent of the bourgeoisie, the family became the center of its value system: all values became reduced to values of the family. And correspondingly, all space was divided, with respect to the family, between an inside and an outside, with a ritual threshold separating them; the inside was the comforting space of the family, the home, rationality, respectability; the outside was the dangerous space outside the family, the place of irrationality, of the pleasures of the body, of adventures. The rise of the novel is umbilically connected to the rise of the bourgeoisie: and it soon became not only the favorite literary expression, but also the privileged way for the bourgeoisie's own imaging and the communication of the norms of its code. In so doing, the novel aims at the elimination of the romance, or at least at its displacement into an area of insignificance and marginality, for the romance deals with the condition of one who is outside the family.[21] But within the parameters of this dichotomy of space, mobility belongs to adventure, to the romance, and as such it is potentially dangerous to the values of the inside and therefore has to be condemned.

The journey toward a demoralizing of mobility will be long and laborious. Values will have to be changed or at least reinterpreted before motion—while still retaining the ability to signify metaphorically—can become merely the ability to change space. In a recent poem by Rodari, that journey appears to have been completed:

> Pulcinella andava a Biella,
> montò sopra una carrozzella,
> e se il cavallo era attaccato
> certo a quest'ora era arrivato.
>
> Pulcinella andava a Torino,
> montò sopra un cavallino,
> e se il cavallo non era di legno
> andava a Torino e anche a Collegno.
>
> [Pulcinella was going to Biella,
> mounted on a horse-drawn cab,
> and if the horse had been in harness
> he surely would have arrived by now.
>
> Pulcinella was going to Turin,
> mounted on a pony,
> and if it hadn't been made of wood
> he'd have gone to Turin and Collegno too.][22]

The only reason for stasis is no longer the moral condemnation of mobility, but simply the lack of a motor.[23]

ITALIE-ITALIES: TYPO/TOPOLOGIES OF FRENCH TRAVEL ACCOUNTS IN THE NINETEENTH CENTURY

Christian Bec

To review in a brief paper all the accounts of French travel in Italy during the nineteenth century is, one must admit, as arduous as it is tantalizing.

Let us consider the obstacles.

First, there is the problem of quantity: the large number of travel accounts that flourished in France and were written in French during this century is remarkable, to say the least (hundreds of texts and thousands of pages printed).[1]

Second, this production is marked by a high degree of heterogeneity not only in terms of authors but also in terms of genres. The authors represented range from famous names such as Chateaubriand, Stendhal, Maupassant, Barrès, to others not as well known, including some who are anonymous.[2]

The range and variety of these writers pose a third difficulty. A distinction should be made between travelers who become authors for the occasion, and authors who undertake to travel. What predominates with the former group is the actual journey, whereas in the latter group, the dominant features are the writing process itself and the relationship the authorial "I" establishes with all that is peculiarly foreign to it.

In addition, the difference in socioprofessional status among writers is as varied as their motivations for these undertakings:[3]

be they for journalistic or educational reasons, as well as for the purpose of entertainment.[4]

Matters are made worse by the wide chronological and cultural differences in the authors. The human perspective between Chateaubriand and Bourget differs widely, for example. Moreover, let us keep in mind the changes these travelers were studying. The early travelers were confronting the social reality of an old country, divided into many small states, struggling to become a nation; the post-1860 writers faced the reality of a young nation, in law more than in fact, struggling to join the occidental family of nations.

From this brief study, it should not come as a surprise, therefore, to see a kaleidoscope of nineteenth-century French travel accounts about Italy.

Can we find a common ground in the present survey? Is it possible for us to establish reliable typo/topological constructs in these widely differing textual labyrinths? The vitality of the genre in France would suggest to us at first glance that the answer to these questions is yes. Writers such as Du Bellay, Rabelais, Montaigne,[5] Montesquieu, De Brosses, and others, who participated in the famous Grand Tour, had already established a well-defined tradition with a wealth of scholarly and specialized works. French travel writers of the period were also well acquainted with foreign writers, such as Byron and Goethe, to mention only two illustrious names. Last but not least, these writers were not strangers to many travel manuals, including older ones such as those produced by Misson, Lalonde, and Saint-Non all of which were readily available.[6]

Let us now proceed to a concrete analysis of the texts in question, and let us begin with a "standard" text, *L'Italia* or the *Voyage en Italie* by Théophile Gautier. This choice is based on the following criteria:

1. Gautier, we feel, is a representative writer of the genre.
2. He traveled to Italy at a crucial period (1850–51), as the country was just beginning its journey toward modernity.[7]
3. He published his travel accounts first in pamphlet form, for

G. Carlini. *La famiglia Tolstoy a Venezia* (The Tolstoy family in Venice). The Hermitage, Saint Petersburg, Russia.

a wider public in the *Presse,* and they were revised later into book form.

4. Having already traveled to Spain and Africa, he was well equipped to write with authority.[8]

In order to restrict further the scope of our study we will focus our attention on one city in Italy: Venice. We do so not only because Gautier accords special privilege to this city, but also because Venice constitutes a microcosm of the country.

How does Gautier view Venice?

Gautier arrives in Venice by train at night after having bypassed the city of Brescia due to a missed stagecoach connection.[9] He obtains a room at the Hotel de l'Europe.[10] His first night in Venice is taken up largely by fending off mosquitoes and by his plans to visit those places in the Venetian countryside he had often admired in paintings.[11] The following morning he discovers typical Venetian scenes with gondolas and gondoliers, which he describes with painstaking exactitude and enthusiasm.[12] While in Venice he does not fail to visit all the famous monuments, including the ghetto.

What catches his interest, however, are the typical scenes and anecdotes: two beggars,[13] a corpulent matron,[14] the well-to-do people,[15] the ragged monks,[16] dark-eyed blondes and brunettes,[17] an orderly demonstration against the occupying Austrians,[18] and the presence of a "naïve foi méridionale" [naive southern faith].[19]

Above all, Venice in the eyes of Gautier appeared to be a fallen city, burdened by its glorious past.[20] At the same time, the writer appreciated the enchanting and fantastic qualities Venice evoked in him during his evening strolls along the city's canals:

> Au haut des arches, des formes vaguement humaines nous regardaient passer comme les mornes figures d'un rêve. Parfois, toutes les lueurs s'éteignaient, et l'on s'avançait sinistrement entre quatre espèces de ténèbres, les ténèbres huileuses, humides et profondes de l'eau, les ténèbres tem-

pêtueuses du ciel nocturne et les ténèbres opaques des deux murailles, sur l'une desquelles la lanterne de la barque jetait un reflet rougeâtre qui révélait des piédestaux, des fûts de colonne, des portiques et des grilles aussitôt disparus. Tous les objets touchés dans cette obscurité par quelque rayon égaré prenaient des apparences mystérieuses, fantastiques, effrayantes, hors de proportion.

[From high on the arches, forms, vaguely human, watched us pass by like dreary figures in a dream. Sometimes, all the lights went out and we advanced sinisterly among four types of shadows, the oily, humid, deep shadows of the water, the stormy shadows of the night sky, and the opaque shadows of the two walls, on one of which the boat's lantern cast a reddish reflection that revealed pedestals, columns, porticos, and grates, which disappeared immediately. All the objects touched in this darkness by some stray ray of light took on an appearance at once mysterious, fantastic, freightening, out of proportion.][21]

The city of Venice evoked, in Gautier, memories of Musset, of De Brosses,[22] of Gozzi,[23] as well as many images that he had accumulated from other travel accounts.[24]

This is the Venice of a writer who is traditionally considered to possess "l'eccezionale capacità di evocare e di descrivere con vivacità di colori, in un linguaggio quanto mai suggestivo paesaggi, monumenti, uomini, costumi" [The exceptional capacity to evoke and to describe landscapes, monuments, men, customs, in living color and in a language more suggestive than ever].[25] This, undoubtedly, is the "true" Venice of the time, which Gautier admits to having painted like a picture.[26]

Following Gautier's footsteps, Chateaubriand also sojourned at the Hotel de l'Europe.[27] As others had done before him (Comines, Dante, Petrarch, Byron), Chateaubriand, while engaging in customary descriptions, added his voice to a long-standing lament against the loss of the "freedom and glory" of the ancient

Republic.[28] A number of other writers echo these feelings. Arsène Houssaye, citing Alfred de Musset, mourns for the past independence. Georges Sand, in a splendid nocturnal scene, remembers Gozzi and decries the oppressive state in which the old Venetian Republic now finds itself.[29] Louise Colet also follows Musset's footsteps to the Hotel Danieli and reflects upon the Venetian landscape.[30] Finally, Hyppolite Taine, who also recalls De Brosses and Gozzi, emphasizes the suggestive power of a nocturnal Venetian scene.[31]

Venice, we might easily infer, is therefore the city of canonical images, from whose charm no talented writer can escape.

Let us for a moment return to Théophile Gautier. Having crossed the border at the Sempion Pass, he, like Chateaubriand before him, discovered, much to his dismay, that Italy was far less "méridionale" than he had expected.[32] At Padua and at Sesto Calende, Gautier, as Quinet before him, was struck by the beautiful women with dark eyes.[33] Florence revealed to him the eternal qualities of the Mediterranean people described by previous authors. Gautier was also struck by the shepherds dressed in typical costumes that he encountered on the slopes of the Apennines. However, the most lasting impression was that of an ubiquitous sense of death permeating the entire country like "a collection of dead cities."[34]

Chateaubriand, instead, who considered himself an artist, a poet, and a philosopher, saw Italy as nothing more than a country symbolizing the decadence of social institutions, reminding one of the brevity of human existence.[35] While in Rome he, in fact, was only drawn to the ancient Christian churches and the Roman ruins. Unlike the originality he displayed in the *Génie du Christianisme*, Chateaubriand managed to reduce his description of Italy to a series of platitudes and time-honored stereotypes. Rome, for example, is associated only with St. Peter's and the Colosseum,[36] Naples only with Mount Vesuvius.[37]

Lamartine himself was no more original when he stated: "Ah le triste pays que l'Italie si on veut y vivre avec les morts" [Oh how sad a country Italy is if one wants to live there among the dead] and "Naples n'est plus Naples" [Naples is no longer Naples]. Other contemporary artists drew from the same stereotypical sources. Dumas became the painter of the poor, of the dispossessed, and of the brigands.[38] Paul de Musset was famous for his sketches of the jettatori [those who cast evil eyes], and Maupassant for his depictions of the dark-eyed beauties.[39]

Why is the image of Italy, as presented by the nineteenth-century authors so far discussed, so arguably stereotypical and ambiguous? Why is the Italy perceived by French travelers always, on the one hand, the land of sorcery and charm, of myth and tradition, of coarseness and poverty, and on the other, a locus amoenus?

The reasons for these contradictory images of Italy are as varied as they are complex. Let us quickly list the main ones.

1. The France that Gautier and his successors represent is at once chauvinistic and xenophobic.[40] The French middle class, taking Paris as its only standard, is consequently suspicious of a country judged to be archaic, stagnant, and at best strange.[41]

2. The writers who traveled to Italy did so with preconceived ideas and attitudes, which they had acquired through previous readings. The journeys they undertook often served, therefore, not to change but to confirm these prejudices.

3. Despite several attempts to do otherwise, the French authors who journeyed to Italy in the nineteenth century followed a fixed itinerary dictated by tourist guides designed to appeal to mass tourism.[42]

4. Finally, as rightly stated as early as 1691 in Misson's *Nouveau voyage/ou guide/d'Italie:* "It is easier to say good things about a recently discovered island or a distant region than a neighbouring country familiar to us."

It may not be unreasonable to construe at this point that we have taken too polemical a position, especially since some italophiles singled out and emphasized negative aspects of Italian life that others may haven chosen to ignore.

However, our point of view is on purpose reductive and tends to privilege repetitions and clichés. Thus, we have not mentioned two fundamental aspects that govern the relationship between Italy and the French writers of the nineteenth century. The first one, introduced by Stendhal, is the discovery of happiness in Italy.

J'y ai réfléchi: je recommencerais mon voyage, si c'était à refaire; non pas que j'aie rien gagné du côté de l'esprit; c'est l'âme qui a gagné. La vieillesse morale est recluée pour moi de dix ans. J'ai senti la possibilité d'un nouveau bonheur. Tous les ressorts de mon âme ont été nourris et fortifiés; je me sens rajeuni. Les gens secs ne peuvent plus rien pour moi: je connais la terre où l'on respire cet *air* céleste dont ils nient l'existence; je suis de fer pour eux.

[I have thought about it: I would start my journey all over, if I could do it again; not that I did not gain anything from the spiritual point of view; it's my soul that gained. A moral old age has been hiding in me for ten years. I felt the possibility of a new happiness. All the energies of my soul have been nourished and fortified; I feel rejuvenated. Those arid people can give me nothing more: I know the land where one can breathe that celestial *air* whose existence they deny; I am made of iron for them.][43]

The other, described by Bourget, is the discovery of oneself, that is, "le travail d'une âme" [the workings of the soul] through the Italian journey.

Elle réside d'abord, cette sensation du voyage, dans ce pourvoir que seule possède l'absence de nous rendre à nousmême. Etre loin, c'est être affranchi de tant de devoirs et de tant de misères, de tant d'habitudes lassantes ou douces! ... Il y a deux efforts également difficiles pour un civilisé et qu'emporte le tourbillon brûlant, desséchant, des cités modernes. ... Vivre sa vraie vie, sentir son vrai "moi," c'est le premier de ces deux efforts. Mettre à leur vraie place les petites misères de sa propre destinée, c'est la second.

[This sensation of traveling resides above all in the power, which belongs to absence alone, of rendering ourselves to ourselves. To be far away is to be set free from so many duties and so many miseries, so many habits either tiring or sweet! . . . There are two efforts equally difficult for a civilized person, brought about by the burning withering turmoil of modern cities. . . . To live one's true life, to feel one's true "self"—that is the first of these two efforts. To put in their proper place the little miseries of one's own destiny, that is the second.][44]

To conclude: In the 1860s, Baedeker triumphs in Europe and becomes a must for all travelers. As we know, the guide was only meant to appeal to the ordinary tourist and purposely omitted details but emphasized those items worthy of greater attention. It was published simultaneously in German, English, and French. Could not this editorial policy mean that the world of tourism in the West was becoming more homogeneous? And could it also not mean perhaps that our French travelers were becoming increasingly more cosmopolitan in outlook?[45]

THE SIGNIFICANCE OF THE JOURNEY IN MANZONI

S. B. Chandler

Although the concept of life as a journey did not reach its full development until *I promessi sposi,* Manzoni had already used it in his early poems. In *Alla Musa* (1802), he asks the Muse to indicate to him a "novo intatto sentier" [new and untraveled path] (p. 165) so that her flame may not be buried in him; if he falls "sul calle ascreo" [on the Ascran road] let it be said that he lies on his own track.¹ The concept is related more closely to his own life in *In morte di Carlo Imbonati* (1805–6). Imbonati says that he had wished to guide Manzoni step by step "su la via scoscesa" [on the steep road] (p. 194) that he himself, panting for breath, had supplied to him. Imbonati tells the poet to follow his road since it did not please him "su la via più trita" [on the most beaten road] (p. 196) to jostle with the crowd that runs after pleasure, vain honor, and lucre; let him pursue his way in company with a few fearless friends and with "la pacata compagnia" [the sober company] (p. 197) of the dead, who are still a source of respect and a guide. Manzoni asks Imbonati to show him the road he can take to touch the summit or to bring it about that, if he falls on the slope, people will at least say that he lies on his own track (a repetition of the expression in *Alla Musa*), Imbonati enjoins him never to take his eyes from the goal. Finally in these early poems, Manzoni assures his readers in *Urania* (1809) that, from the first steps "Nel terrestre viaggio ove il desio / Crudel compagno è de la via" [On the earthly journey where desire / is the road's cruel companion] (p. 201), a deep love suggests to him that one day Italy, the abode of the ancient Muses, may number him among the sacred group of her bards.

In the *Inni Sacri*, references to life as a journey are almost nonexistent. In *La Risurrezione* (April 1812), however, when his soul has returned to him, Christ casts away the marble of his tomb like "il pellegrino" [the pilgrim] (p. 12) who, while resting in the forest, returns slowly to consciousness when he feels a dried leaf on his face.

In *Il cinque maggio* (1821), Napoleon while in exile on the island of St. Helena, contemplates his past in despair. He remembers his lightning journeys across Europe: "Di quel securo il fulmine / Tenea dietro al baleno" [From that seclusion the thunder / Came close behind the lightning] (p. 103) and the rapid obedience to his commands. Posterity will decide whether it was true glory, but we bow to the "Massimo Fattor, che volle in lui / Del creator suo spirito / Piú vasta orma stampar" [Greatest Maker, who wanted to see / His creative spirit / Leave a greater mark] (p. 104). Napoleon dominates his age, and his voice seems like that of destiny. The manner and the framework in which he remembers those lightning journeys—now he is pondering the real destination of life—do not permit him to narrate his achievements for posterity: "E sull'eterne pagine / Cadde la stanca man!" [And on the eternal pages / Fell the tired hand] (p. 105); but a hand comes down from heaven:

> E l'avviò, pei floridi
> Sentier della speranza
> Ai campi eterni, al premio
> Che i desideri avanza,
> Dov'è silenzio e tenebre
> La gloria che passò. (pp. 105–6)

> [And sent him down the flourishing
> Paths of hope
> To the eternal fields, to the reward
> That drives the desires,
> Where there is silence and darkness
> The glory that is gone.]

The rapid journeys of his lifetime were of no avail compared to the movement toward heaven upon his repentance, since these journeys were unrelated to life's goal and thus without meaning.

In the tragedy *Il Conte di Carmagnola* (1819), the protagonist looks to chance rather than to personal responsibility. Addressing the Doge and the Venetian Senate he exclaims:

> Oh! beato colui cui la fortuna
> Cosí distinte in suo cammin presenta
> Le vie del biasmo e dell'onor, ch'ei puote
> Correr certo del plauso, e non dar mai
> Passo ove trovi a malignar l'intento
> Sguardo del suo nemico. (p. 308)

> [Oh blessed is he to whom fortune,
> In his path, so distinctly presents
> The ways of blame and of honor, that he may
> Proceed certain of praise, and never give quarter
> Wherever he finds the unremitting
> Stare of his enemy bent on evil.]

It is not the ways of blame or honor that matter in this life, but the road to virtue. Senator Marco, who has set his duty to the Senate above his moral duty to warn Carmagnola of the deceit leading to his execution, soliloquizes:

> Io li ringrazio; ei m'hanno
> Statuito un destino; ei m'hanno spinto
> Per una via; vi corro: almen mi giova
> Ch'io non la scelsi: io nulla scelgo; e tutto
> Ch'io faccio è volontà d'altrui. (p. 366)

> [I thank them; they have given
> Me a destiny; they have pushed me
> Along a path; along which I run; at least it is to my advantage
> That I did not choose it; I choose nothing; and everything
> I do is the will of others.]

He is being sent elsewhere: "in fra i perigli / Certo per sua pietade il cielo m'invia" [in among the perils / Surely for its mercy heaven sends me]. For Manzoni, no one can be thrust along an immoral road that he has not chosen, and Marco could have entered a moral road despite his political oath of secrecy to the Venetian Senate. He assigns to the will of heaven the Senate's decision to post him to an official position far away.

In Manzoni's other tragedy, *Adelchi*, Ermengarda—rejected by her husband Carlo—tells her sister, the abbess Ansberga, that we must journey along the entire road on which heaven has placed us, to its final point, no matter what kind of road it may be. She attributes to heaven, therefore, the consequences of Carlo's action, but Manzoni certainly believed that we must accept a course we cannot change and must entrust ourselves to the consolations offered by Christianity, since our performance in this life determines the nature of the next. In this tragedy, the journey of Martino, the Deacon of Ravenna, provides Carlo with the means of outflanking the Lombard military positions, but I do not identify in it any spiritual significance, even if Carlo, for political reasons, judges it a divine favor.

The *Osservazioni sulla morale cattolica* of 1819 marks a basic point in Manzoni's Christian thought.[2] This life is a preparation for the next, "siamo in cammino" [we are on a journey] (p. 504), so that nothing is stable here below. Because the "secolo presente" [this century] does not have its completion in itself, it is certain that—when in order to follow justice there is no other way than death—God has marked out that way for us to reach him. Religion introduces the idea of instability into every one of our judgments about temporal things, with the necessity of abandoning them; that is, life is a journey through time to death. Man can go over his past in his memory but cannot change it, and "L'idea del tempo che scorre irreparabilmente" [The notion of time passing by inexorably] (p. 472) is accompanied by painful memories. Yet he who is admitted to penitence is on the "via della virtù" [path of virtue] and can change the meaning of his past:

egli comincia di nuovo a battere quella via con alacrità,
con tanto piú di fervore quanto piú si ricorda che frutti
amari ha colti in quella del vizio, quanto piú egli sente che
gli atti e i sentimenti virtuosi sono i mezzi che la religione
gli presenta per crescere nella fiducia che i suoi vestigj su
quella trista via sono cancellati. (p. 340)

[With determination he begins to travel that road again,
the more fervently he does so the more he remembers what
bitter fruits he gathered along the road of vice; even more
so as he realizes that virtuous acts and feelings are the
means religion accords him in order to grow in the faith
that the traces of those sad ways are erased.]

When a person reviews his past and regrets what he has neglected to do, religion "lo consola col fargli conoscere ch'egli è in tempo di cominciare la sola via necessaria alla vera e perpetua felicità" [consoles him with the knowledge that he is in time to start out on the only path necessary for true and eternal happiness] (p. 559). We can turn to this road at any time, but not without an accompanying moral feeling.

Different kinds of roads are possible in this life, but we do not know their nature beforehand. For example, the workings of justice have been depicted to people: "come una via piana e sparsa di fiori, gli è stato detto che non si trattava che di scegliere fra i piaceri; ed ora si trova fra il piacere e la giustizia, fra un gran dolore e una grande iniquità" [as a road that is flat and covered with flowers, he has been told that it was not a matter of choosing between pleasures, and now he finds himself between pleasures and justice, between a great pain and a great iniquity] (p. 394). We cannot take a step without finding the Gospel on our road: people pretend not to see it, they can dodge it and try not to come in contact with it, at least in words, but not in fact. Our road is sometimes impeded by others, who place before us a "pietra d'inciampo" [stumbling block] (p. 507); we can avoid it or cast it from our path but we shall not be excused if we fall, though it remains a great evil to place stumbling blocks before others. The true way to return to God involves a change of heart and of mode of life, a repairing of evils committed, and a faith in God who can save:

> E questa è la via per cui ci conduce la Chiesa; è quella su cui corrono i semplici colla sicurezza di che si sente condotto da una mano pietosa e sicura; su cui sono corsi e corrono tanti ingegni illuminati, i quali veggendo che tutto fuori di questa è precipizio, sono tanto più umili, tanto più riconoscenti, quanto più sono illuminati. (p. 337)

> [And this is the way along which the Church leads us; this is the one along which the simple folk travel with the certainty of those who feel they are led by a steady and merciful hand; along which have traveled and are traveling many enlightened minds who, seeing that everything outside this is a void, are that much more humble, that much more grateful, that much more enlightened.]

Before examining the motif of the journey in *I promessi sposi*, we may note that in the Lettre à M. Chauvet Manzoni refers to "la marche des événements" [the course of events] (p. 317) and "la marche de l'esprit humain" [the course of the human spirit] (p. 379).[3] Human beings exist in time and so does their history; thus, since their history consists of their actions, it is a record of movement, though not a well-defined journey toward a specific goal. Similarly, we may note, the action of a tragedy, since it is based on human actions, proceeds quickly or slowly.

In *I promessi sposi*, Manzoni goes beyond the general idea of life as a journey.[4] He identifies different types of journeys for different individuals. These journeys stem from the events of the story and from their effects upon the characters, who exist in the specific political and social conditions of northern Italy in the early seventeenth century. Manzoni is far from depicting the wanderings of a man or a woman through various countries—with a succession of adventures involving love affairs, crimes, and meetings with different types of people, as in many novels of the eighteenth century, the age in which the upper class indulged in the Grand Tour. Journeys are frequent for example in Sir Walter Scott's historical novels, and critics have explored the links between Jeanie Deans's journey to London and similar travels in *I promessi sposi*. In this study, I omit comparisons with other works, however, since my purpose is to identify Manzoni's use of the journey and to show its deep significance in his work. The journeys enable Manzoni to present ways humble people are affected by the weakness of government, the power of the local lords, the impact of social conditions, and by details of specific events, such as the famine and the resultant rioting in Milan, and the plague. At the same time, he can use these journeys to permit a character to develop in both a worldly and spiritual sense. Physical movement through space is accompanied by spiritual development in time, though this development—as in the case of Don Rodrigo after Fra Cristoforo's visit—may involve reversion to a previous condition. Renzo, Lucia, and Agnese undertake a literal journey from their village and are described as "viaggiatori" [travelers] (p. 142) when they leave Fra Cristoforo's monastery, since their previous stability has been destroyed forever. Later they will have to reestablish themselves elsewhere, but their individual journeys end in a new stability at a higher economic level in society.

Much critical attention has been paid to Renzo's journey, which has been described as a pilgrimage. Unlike Lucia whose moral and religious conviction is already established, Renzo must experience many vicissitudes before reaching her position, a result symbolized by his forgiveness of Don Rodrigo and his reunion with her in the *lazzeretto,* under the direction of Fra Cristoforo. Before the intervention of Don Rodrigo, Renzo— "nel sentiero retto e piano di vita percorso da lui fin allora" [on the flat straight path of life he had followed until then] (p. 98)— found no occasion to sharpen his brain. Now the direction of his life has changed and he, the unsophisticated countryman, goes to the city. The break between past and future occurs when he looks back at the Resegone and then "tristamente si voltò, e seguitò la sua strada. A poco a poco cominciò poi a scoprir campanili e torri e cupole e tetti" [he turned sadly and continued on his way. Little by little, he then began to discover spires and towers and cupolas and rooftops] (p. 203). At Milan, he not only witnesses the rioting, but learns how to deal with the authorities: for this purpose, one does not openly preach justice but practices the same deceit as they themselves. As the host of the Luna Piena inn ruminates to the sleeping Renzo: "E pretendi girare il mondo, e parlare; e non sai che, a voler far a modo suo, e impiparsi delle gride, la prima cosa è di parlarne con gran riguardo" [And you expect to travel around and talk, and you do not know that, wanting to do things your own way and not giving a care for the decrees, the first thing is to be very careful in the way you talk about them] (p. 261). Renzo descends morally at Milan and goes through Purgatory as he "Cammina, cammina" [walks and walks] (p. 277) toward the Adda, the friend, the brother, the savior: he is the "povero pellegrino" [poor pilgrim] (p. 292). Renzo learns more of the world on his return to Milan during the plague and also of the highest human and religious feelings from Cecilia's mother. As we have seen, he completes his Christian ascent in the *lazzeretto*. On this occasion, Fra Cristoforo's words are revealing; if the Church gives Renzo and Lucia as companions:

> lo fa per avviarvi tutt'e due sulla strada della consolazione che non avrà fine. Amatevi come compagni di viaggio, con questo pensiero d'avere a lasciarvi, e con la speranza di ritrovarvi per sempre. Ringraziate il cielo che v'ha condotti a questo stato non per mezzo dell'allegrezze turbolente e passeggiere, ma co' travagli e tra le miserie, per disporvi a una allegrezza raccolta e tranquilla. (p. 638)
>
> [She does it to start you both off on the never-ending road of consolation. Love each other like traveling companions knowing that you will separate and also with the hope that

you will find each other for ever. Thank heaven that it has led you to this stage not through disorderly and transitory merrymaking, but through trials and tribulations, to prepare you for a tranquil and collected contentment.]

As Renzo departs from the *lazzeretto:*

> Andava dunque il nostro viaggiatore allegramente, senza aver disegnato né dove, né come, né quando, né se avesse da fermarsi la notte, premuroso soltanto di portarsi avanti, d'arrivar presto al suo paese, di trovar con chi parlare, a chi raccontare, soprattutto di poter presto rimettersi in cammino per Pasturo, in cerca d'Agnese. (p. 642)

> [So our traveler continued merrily along, without planning either where or how or when or whether he had somewhere to stay for the night, eager only to keep moving on, to reach his own town soon, to find people to talk to and recount his stories, and above all to be able to get back soon on the road for Pasturo, in search of Agnes.]

His journey now becomes purely physical, because his spiritual progress is complete.

Like Renzo, Agnese and Lucia become travelers from their village since their journey through life is transformed by Don Rodrigo, but their travels lack the deeper meaning of Renzo's. Lucia's journey to the castle of the Innominato [Unnamed] after her kidnapping by his *bravi* [thugs] is fundamental, however, in the resolution of the novel. Manzoni describes the isolation of this castle and makes it clear that only those loyal to the Innominato could go there: it was the center and the rendezvous of sin. Lucia's journey to the castle introduces a new element; on the way, her religious attitude strikes il Nibbio [The Kite], but her Christian position furnishes an example to the Innominato of the effect religion can have on one's life, and thus of the possibilities for him in his moment of spiritual torment when he realizes that life is a journey unto death. The joy and mutual friendliness of those on their way to see Cardinal Borromeo introduce an element of wonder into his mind. He is thus prompted to make his physical and spiritual journey to the cardinal and so to end his isolation. Subsequently, people from the vicinity can go to his castle during the descent of the *lanzichenecchi* [pikemen]. The Innominato tells his *bravi* that "la strada per la quale siamo andati finora, conduce nel fondo dell'inferno" [the road we have been traveling so far leads to the depths of hell] (p. 424). While waiting for the arrival of Lucia whose coach is approaching, the Innominato is unconsciously abandoning that road, but he has not yet decided on the road he will in future follow; thus "si mise a camminare innanzi e indietro per la stanza, con un passo di viaggiatore frettoloso" [he started to pace back and forth in the room with the step of a hurried traveler] (p. 352).

After his interview with Fra Cristoforo, Don Rodrigo "misurava innanzi e indietro, a passi lunghi, quella sala, dalle pareti della quale pendevano ritratti di famiglia, di varie generazioni" [walked back and forth, with long strides, in that room where many family portraits spanning many gnerations hanged] (p. 110). He resolves his movements—which have no definite goal but symbolize an inner conflict—by a physical journey to a certain house, and en route he receives the obsequious respect of those he meets. Later, while waiting for the return of il Griso and his *bravi* and also, he hopes, of Lucia, he "camminava innanzi e indietro, al buio, per una stanzaccia disabitata dell'ultimo piano, che rispondeva sulla spianata" [walked back and forth, in the dark, in a dingy uninhabited room on the last floor that looked out onto an open space] (p. 190). After the failure of the expedition, he continues on the road of sin and decides to solicit the help of the Innominato. Manzoni quotes the supposed manuscript of the Anonimo [Anonymous]:

La strada dell'iniquità, dice qui il manoscritto, è larga; ma questo non vuol dire che sia comoda: ha i suoi intoppi, i suoi passi scabrosi; è noiosa la sua parte, e faticosa, benché vada all'ingiú. . . .

A Don Rodrigo, il quale non voleva uscirne, né dare addietro, né fermarsi, e non poteva andare avanti da sé, veniva bensí in mente un mezzo con cui potrebbe. (p. 310)

[The road of iniquity is wide, the manuscript says here; but this does not mean it is comfortable: it has its stumbling blocks, its rough passages; it is boring in some places, and tiring, even though it goes downhill. . . . To Don Rodrigo, who did not want to get off the road nor go back, nor stop, and who could not go forward on his own, there came to mind a means with which he could find a way out.]

Don Rodrigo's traveling on the road of iniquity now assumes the material form of a journey to the castle of the Innominato. After the Innominato's meeting with Cardinal Borromeo and his repentance, Don Rodrigo avoids meeting the cardinal, who is about to visit the nearby village, by taking a journey to Milan. Don Rodrigo remains on the road of iniquity: the Innominato departs from it by going to meet the cardinal. By his decision, Don Rodrigo exposes himself to the plague in Milan: his continued journey on the way of sin leads to his death.

Gertrude right from her birth is on the way to becoming a nun. When she was a girl at the convent "la faccenda camminava" [things were moving along] (p. 157); then, after having written a letter to her father and after having agreed to take the veil, "ciò che, anche suo malgrado, s'impossessava di tutto il suo animo, era il sentimento de' gran progressi che aveva fatti, in quella giornata, sulla strada del chiostro" [what possessed her entire soul, even against her will, was the feeling of the great progress she had made, that day, on the road to the convent] (p. 172). She had not chosen that way of life of her own free will, but she could have profited from her forced decision because the Christian religion: "È una strada cosí fatta che, da qualunque laberinto, da qualunque precipizio, l'uomo capiti ad essa, e vi faccia un passo, può d'allora in poi camminare con sicurezza e di buona voglia, e arrivar lietamente a un lieto fine" [It is a road that, from whatever labyrinth or precipice a man happens across it and steps on it, he can from then on walk ahead with safety and alacrity and arrive happily to a good end] (p. 183). Subsequently, Gertrude "tentò tutte le strade per esimersi dall'orribile comando" [attempted in every way to evade the terrible command] of Egidio to send Lucia forth to be kidnapped by the *bravi* of the Innominato: "tutte, fuorché la sola ch'era sicura, e che le stava pur sempre aperta davanti" [in every way, except the only one that was certain and that was still open to her] (pp. 343–44). In all circumstances of our lives, the Christian road lies open before us.

Don Abbondio at the beginning of the novel is physically walking along the road. He has, from an early age, viewed his life as a journey: he is "come un vaso di terra cotta, costretto a viaggiare in compagnia di molti vasi di ferro" [like a terracotta vase, forced to travel in the company of many iron vases] (p. 19) and has thus adopted a certain code of behavior. During his walk, the two *bravi* of Don Rodrigo accost him, and he laments "vedete se quelle due figuracce, dovevan proprio piantarsi sulla mia strada, e prenderla con me" [see if those two thugs really have to plant themselves in my way and make trouble for me] (p. 21): the literal road is equivalent to the road of life and there is no exit from it to right or left, Don Abbondio must go forward physically and spiritually. Ironically, shortly after the Innominato's conversion and the complete change in his way of life, he and Don Abbondio become "i due compagni di viaggio" [two traveling companions] (p. 393) on their way to his castle; for the Innominato it is a journey to complete his conversion by the release of Lucia, for Don Abbondio an annoyance and a mere obedience to the order of the archbishop.

For Manzoni, then, life is a journey through time. The nature of that journey depends on the conditions in which we live and, within the journey, the individual will make various subsidiary journeys, which cannot be separated from the main journey; some of these may be misguided and conflict with the goal of life, others will deepen our understanding of human life and society. We cannot control the circumstances of our lives, but we can choose the road of religion of our own free will, no matter how great the difficulties. Our destination is in the next life, beyond time.[5]

Seven

VERGA, OR THE IMPOSSIBLE JOURNEY

Romano Luperini

The changeability of the chronotope (literally, time-space) is a constant in travel literature.¹ The variations in the landscape that unfolds before the traveler's eyes depend upon the time frames of the journey itself.

In the age of modernity the relationship between elements of the chronotope tends to assume unique characteristics. This is due not only to the greater velocity of the journey, but also to the profound transformation undergone by the concept of time, which becomes linear space at once delimited and discreet and therefore divisible into progressive units. It is within this new concept of space that we should consider the notion of journey time.

The obsessive quantification of time and space is unique to modernity. The epic is not concerned with the linearity of time but rather with its cyclical characteristics. Within this temporal framework, even the journey tends to take on the circular rhythm of eternal recurrence. The epic-lyrical rhythm of departure already alludes to that of return.

If the circular movement of the relationship between human life and nature and the merging of life and destiny in Greek and Latin epics defines the return journeys or the discovery of a new homeland, today such notions seem remote and impracticable. The idea of the medieval pilgrim who descends into hell or ascends Mount Purgatory to reach a meaning and a purpose outside of worldly coordinates is today just as inconceivable. So, can the modern quantification of time and space (based as it is on economic rationality) still provide any meaning to the metaphor of the journey? Both classical and Christian epics presuppose an itinerary leading to a homeland, a journey endowed with value and meaning. Is it possible for the novel, within the context of modernity, to recapture the meaning of this metaphor? Verga provides a reply to this question, and his answer is no.

In *I Malavoglia*, the premodern and modern worlds come face to face. The universe inhabited by the Toscano family is (Bakhtin would argue) that of the idyllic or familiar novel. Within such a universe, the village of Trezza still conveys the idea of a protective nest, watched over by the periodic return of the constellations and by the reassuring rumble of the sea. Time is folkloristic, marked by the cycle of seasons and of harvests; space is delineated by a virginal nature that, albeit undermined by progress, can still provide a direct and authentic refuge. A direct relationship with nature's manifestations is still possible. Nevertheless, this universe is surrounded by fear and the unknown; beyond its boundaries the only possibilities are those of displacement and vagabondage. There are "strade arse di sole e bianche di polvere" [roads baked by the sun and white with dust] (p. 596) where carts rumble along and vagabonds roam excluded from the protection and familiar intimacy of the village; there are the awesome and mysterious harbors that lure 'Ntoni and from which Nunziata's father never comes back; there are the big cities where the fever of progress pulsates, where Lia falls by the wayside and Master 'Ntoni dies. Those who leave the village are destined either never to return, or to return as strangers only to realize that they should never have left, or returned. Beyond the boundaries of Trezza a different world exists, a world governed by a different consciousness of time, of space, and of their relationship—the modern world. Between the two worlds no communication is possible. Between the first and the second, in fact, there lies the empty space of an alternative that allows no compromise but demands instead a resolute choice involving reciprocal exclusion: to leave Trezza is to undergo symbolically the experience of death. This explains why, in *I Malavoglia*, although the topos of the journey is always present as a sense of foreboding, the journey itself is never fully reconstructed. What is done, instead, is to describe many departures but few returns. The few characters who return do so at the expense of complete estrangement. The only one who tries time and again to set out on a journey is 'Ntoni, who more than all the other characters fits the novel's structure, being the most firmly planted in the temporal dimension of the modern world. Instead, Master 'Ntoni belongs to the immobility of the epic: his departure, at the end of the novel, represents only the beginning of his journey toward death. Luca and Lia leave forever; Alfio, who had gone to Bicocca to seek his fortune, returns only to experience the absurdity of both his departure and his return.

In *I Malavoglia*, the boundary between the premodern world and the modern one is also the boundary between the epic and the novel, between cyclical time and linear time, between the confined sacred space of the village and the open profane space of the city. The journey as both duration and distance is nowhere represented, since representing it in such a manner would entail a journey leading from the archaic-rural world to the modern one and would therefore signify the profanation of a boundary. The horizon of the premodern world can be defined only by means of renunciation, sacrifice, and self-repression; it looms large and is symbolically exorcised rather than dealt with and resolved realistically. Even the meticulous care with which the novel rigorously respects the unity of place forms part of this exorcism.

The last pages of *I Malavoglia* clearly exemplify how the topos of the journey coincides with the relationship between the premodern and the modern worlds. Like his previous absences from the village, 'Ntoni's life away from the village remains outside the boundaries of narrative space. The silence with which the author treats these absences becomes more effective and forceful than any explicit condemnation. 'Ntoni returns a foreigner, only to utter his last farewell. Even Alfio (a few pages earlier), shortly after his return from Bicocca, proclaimed: "Quando uno lascia il suo paese è meglio che non ci torni piú" [When you leave your village, it is much better if you never come back] (p. 584).

'Ntoni's farewell to Trezza is a farewell to the civilization of the eternal recurrence. In the last chapter, Verga compares Alessi with 'Ntoni in order to suggest two opposite destinies: Alessi's is characterized by home-refuge and village-nest; 'Ntoni's by the displacement of exile and progress. The treacherous sea that always mutters the same old story, the *Tre Re* that glitter in the sky, the *Puddara* that heralds dawn, all belong to the patriarchal universe that Alessi represents and that his brother is forced to abandon forever. As a new dawn is about to break, 'Ntoni looks back for the last time at the village, the sky, and the sea. The beginning of a new day becomes part of the reassuring rhythm from which he has been definitively excluded. Everything returns and repeats itself as always. Even the narrator's words and phrases are repeated with an epic lyrical cadence: the expression "to begin" is reiterated seven times, whereas the phrase "a cominciar la sua giornata" [to begin his day's work] (p. 598) appears three times. Rocco Spatu, too, belongs to this cyclical time. The last so-called problematic reference to this character ("Ma il primo di tutti a cominciar la sua giornata è stato Rocco Spatu" [But Rocco Spatu was the first to begin the day's work] {p. 598}) has been defined by many critics as being devoid of sense and meaning. In reality, such interpretation does not consider that, although Rocco Spatu occupies the bottom rung of the social ladder, at that point he is seen to be a harmonious part of the idyllic and familiar universe that 'Ntoni is obliged to reject forever. Rocco Spatu can "begin his day's work," just as Uncle Santoro and the fishing boats had done a few minutes earlier. (However, Mangiacarrubbe and Brasi Cipolla had already become the objects of 'Ntoni's painful envy because "andranno a dormire nella loro casa" [they will go to sleep in their own home] {p. 597}). Rocco Spatu's movements are linked to the use of the imperfect tense, which is also reserved, in these last pages, for the constellations, the sea, the boats, and the life in the village. This is a durative tense that underlines repetition and continuity, the natural flow of the seasons and daily human activities that, beginning at dawn, follow one another, generation after generation. 'Ntoni's tense, instead, is the past absolute, the tense of definitiveness and completion. The juxtaposition of these two tenses emphasizes the dissonance between two different ways of conceiving the relationship between time and space and, consequently, between two separate chronotopes. In fact, from here onward, Verga follows 'Ntoni in his journey into the modern world, thereby replacing the idyllic and familiar novel with the novel "about trials and tribulations." The author abandons the imperfect for the past absolute, myth for history, and the cult of the family for the logic of "roba."

This is why 'Ntoni's farewell is marked by the tragic tone of a historic event. He who knows everything (this new awareness is reasserted twice in the last pages) also knows that integration would have been possible only within Trezza; he also knows this is no longer possible, so his destiny is simply to accept the alienation of the linear time of progress and of big cities. It is important, at this juncture, to note the heightened dimension of the biographical reference. Through 'Ntoni the author symbolically celebrates the rejection of his previous romantic formation, which had made him search for a moment of "fresh and serene meditation" in the archaic-rural world, in the hope of finding alternative values within its framework.[2] The end of the novel marks the termination of Verga's romantic anticapitalistic stance. The idealization of the village-family ("si sentiva chiacchierare per tutto il paese, come fossimo tutti una famiglia" [You could hear a hubbub of voices coming from the village, as if we were all one big family] {p. 597}) is projected toward the past. Memory here nostalgically transfigures the realities of village life, which are, as the reader knows, steeped in pettiness, as well as in social and economic tensions, and completely dominated by cynicism and the logic of profit. The myth of Trezza does not belong to the boundaries of the present but only to those of memory. Memory and symbols bridge the fractures that "verismo" had already so mercilessly portrayed. Thus Trezza can become the land of a remote civilization, where the relationship with nature can still be fulfilling and authentic.

The archaic-rural universe idealized by memory still permits not only the symbolic lyricism of the *correspondances* between the characters' soul and the universe, but also the epic cadence that marks the proverbs uttered by Master 'Ntoni—a character in whom internal and external, humanity and destiny, perfectly coincide, exactly as in the epic. After *I Malavoglia*, the authenticity of a direct relationship with nature will become more difficult. The symbolic and lyrical solutions will become progressively fewer until they disappear completely in *Vagabondaggio*. Whereas the heroes resemble 'Ntoni rather than Master 'Ntoni, the protagonists of Verga's later phase (such as Gesualdo, or Bianca, or Diodata) are indeed characterized by an excess of humanity despite their harsh fate and, quite often, by a lacerating contradiction between internal and external, between feelings and economic forces. They reflect, in other words, the narrative demands of the new bourgeois novel, in so far as they are no longer a part of the immobility and the rituals of the epic.

'Ntoni's farewell takes us into the secular and profane world of the age of modernity.

Before *Mastro-don Gesualdo*, the road leading from the premodern world to the modern one gives Verga the possibility of a rest. Perhaps the accumulation of wealth in a rural world still affords him a pause in the ever-widening spiral of the epic rhythm typical of the premodern world.

Verga sets out on his new journey in the world of "roba," in the guise of a wayfarer, as can be seen in the opening sentence of the short story *La roba* (Property): "Il viandante che andava lungo il Biviere di Lentini . . ." [the traveler who was going along the lake of Lentini . . .] (p. 636). It seems as if an epic-lyrical tone is still possible, whereas naturalism can suddenly become a sort of anthropocentric panism typical of symbolism:

> E verso sera, allorché il sole tramontava rosso come il fuoco, e la campagna si velava di tristezza, si incontravano le lunghe file degli aratri di Mazzarò che tornavano adagio adagio dal maggese, e i buoi che passavano il guado lentamente, col muso nell'acqua scura. . . . Tutta roba di Mazzarò. Pareva che fosse di Mazzarò perfino il sole che tramontava, e le cicale che ronzavano, e gli uccelli che andavano a rannicchiarsi col volo breve dietro le zolle, e il sibilo dell'assiolo nel bosco. Pareva che Mazzarò fosse disteso tutto grande per quanto era grande la terra, e che gli si camminasse sulla pancia.

> [And toward evening, as the sun was setting red as fire, and the countryside was putting on a veil of sadness, one would see the long lines of Mazzarò's ploughs returning very slowly from the fallow land and the oxen crossing the ford languidly with their muzzles in the dark water. All Mazzarò's property. It seemed that everything was Mazzarò's even as far as the setting sun, and the buzzing cicadas, and the birds darting back to hide themselves behind the clouds, and the hooting of the horned owl in the woods. It seemed as if Mazzarò was spread out as wide as the earth was wide and one was walking across his belly.] (p. 636)

Even in this short story, we can already see the first signs of the transformation undergone by nature, which indeed, tends to become a part of the landscape of property. From this point onward, from the *Novelle rusticane* to *Vagabondaggio* and to *Mastro-don Gesualdo*, the stars never reappear, the *Tre Re* and the *Puddara* stop glittering, the rumble of the sea is heard no more. In *Vagabondaggio* and in *Mastro*, nature no longer belongs to humanity. What belongs to people is only the rural landscape.

"A second nature," Marx would have said, to describe the landscape of the modern world.

In this new landscape, there is no village, no intimacy, no protection. Only vagabondage, so dreaded and cursed by the Malavoglia, prevails: only wandering here and there in pursuit of the dream of profit and property. The opening part of the short story that gives its title to the collection *Vagabondaggio* announces the rejection of the epic and symbolic lyricism, and the descent into the misery of a world without myths, marked not so much by the repetition of the periodic cycles of the constellations as by repetition of human struggles for the bare necessities of a life now deprived of its aura: "Passavano carri, passavano vetturali, passava gente a piedi e a cavallo d'ogni paese, e se ne andavano pel mondo, di qua e di là del fiume" [carts went by, carriages went by, people on foot and on horseback went by, from everywhere, and they all went out into the world, from this and that side of the river] (p. 819).

Vagabondage is what fate has in store for Nanni, the character supposed to portray Gesualdo's childhood and adolescence in the initial project of *Mastro*. The idea of writing a Bildungsroman was eventually discarded and the draft was turned into a short story entitled *Vagabondaggio*. Verga's project of writing about the protagonist's formation or education was dropped. From the very start, Nanni appears before us as an "educated" adult, for he is completely at one with the world of property and economic interests. To Nanni, traveling does not entail his abandoning himself to the picaresque pleasures of an adventurous life, but rather it is the metaphorical manifestation of his alienation from affection and homeland, of his total displacement from a reified world that has transformed the individual into its own image. To the estrangement of the "I" corresponds the estrangement of the landscape; to the absence of the character's inner world corresponds the disappearance of harmony between humans and nature, which no longer retains its former magic. One does not depart anymore; one does not return. Thus, journeys are no longer possible; what remains is the aimless wandering. Vagabondage, which in *I Malavoglia* was a fate reserved only for 'Ntoni, is now a condition common to all the characters.

If in *I Malavoglia* the path leading from the premodern to the modern world is not possible and journeys can not take place within its narrative space, in *Mastro*, instead, journeys are an integral part of the productive infrastructure of the modern epoch. Moreover, in the last part of *Mastro*, journeys represent an attempt, though vain and desperate, either to escape from disease or to search for a cure. Gesualdo's journeys—to Giolio, to Camemi, and to Canziria in part 1, chapter 4, as well as the one in the ensuing chapter to the Torretta toward Fiumegrande—are all attempts to escape from disease. The journey to Mangalavite, which he makes in the absurd hope of being cured in the country air, or the last one from Vizzini to his son-in-law's palace in Palermo, where he goes to convalesce, are to be seen instead as means to search for ephemeral cures.

In *Mastro*, the chronotope seems to have undergone a profound transformation with respect to the chronotope previously advanced in *I Malavoglia*. The new novel lacks both mythological and idyllic moments. Time is quickened, relentless, feverish. The lingering pace that characterizes the short story *La roba* whose rhythm is lyrically expressed by means of the past progressive tense, is no longer possible. Time is linear and fragmented. Its speed is not fluid but irregular, subdivided into critical segments in which actions narrated by means of the absolute past are dramatically condensed. Gesualdo's notion of time is defined by that of production. His day is not a time to be lived, but rather a period to be segmented according to the laws of productive forces.

This is exactly what happens in chapters 4 and 5 of part 1. From the very beginning of chapter 4, we are faced with two different notions of time: that of Gesualdo, which affords no respite, and that of all the other characters, which is more relaxed and conducive to lingering and rest. The more Gesualdo's race against time is slowed by obstacles placed in his path, the more feverish it becomes. Even the landscape (as we shall see) constitutes an obstacle. He has to make haste for, as he says, "ci ho ancora i covoni sull'aia!" [I still have my sheaves in the yard!] (p. 968). He has to visit the Giolio olive mill, go back to the village, supervise the construction of the Camemi road, and see to the farming on the Canziria property, where the sheaves and the wheat are waiting for him to be threshed. Continuous chronological references indicate the implacable aspect of time. Before noon, having traveled all the way from Vizzini to Giolio and having visited the mill, he declares that he has to stop at Camemi, and "ci vogliono due ore" [it takes two hours] (p. 970). He then goes back to the village, along a steep slope and across a barren and scorched landscape, and gets there as the clock strikes twelve. After having met Father Lupi, after having quarreled with his brother-in-law, after having argued with Pirtuso, while his interlocutors are intent on having lunch, Gesualdo goes back to the post office, and from there, under the blazing midday sun and across the red-hot Petrajo gorge, he reaches the road under construction in Camemi, only to set out once again. He "finally" reaches Canziria: "erano circa due ore di notte" [it took two hours traveling at night] (p. 975). The same feverish rhythm marks the next chapter, which begins with the verb to run ("Masi, il garzone, corse a svegliare don Gesualdo" [Masi, the farm boy, ran to wake up Gesualdo] {p. 982}). It continues with a description of the frantic Gesualdo, who "col viso al vento, frustato dalla burrasca, spronava sempre la mula" [with his face to the wind, whipped by the storm, kept spurring the mule] (p. 983) toward Fiumegrande and from there to the village in order to discuss with Father Lupi the business of the bridge.

Unlike the vagabondage of the 1887 collection, Gesualdo's frenetic movements are not without destination; and yet, they are marked by the same sort of estrangement and cruel absurdity. A number of anonymous characters—whose narrative function is to convey, either directly or indirectly, such a message to the reader—appears on the scene. The first is an old man who, after having met Gesualdo under the blazing sun just before the village, exclaims: "O dove andate vossignoria a quest'ora? . . . Avete tanti denari, e vi date l'anima al diavolo!" [Where are you going, sir, at this time of the day? . . . You have so much money, and you sell your soul to the devil!] (p. 970). The theme of money (and of selling and buying) is associated with the idea of selling one's soul to the devil: the infernal landscape that Gesualdo traverses with such difficulty corresponds to the landscape of his internal life, marked by a fatal exchange, the soul for wealth. In the age of "Banks and Industrial Enterprises" (as defined by Verga in the preface to *Eva*), the *intérieur* is completely subordinate to the *comptoir:* this is the modern world's real pact with the devil.

Later on, as Gesualdo leaves the village, the author's comment on Gesualdo's day's work is already implicit in the scene's montage, but this does not make it less cruel: an old farmer suffering from malaria is waiting to meet Gesualdo, in the hope of selling his olives. Gesualdo "lasciò cadere un'offerta minima, seguitando ad andarsene per la sua strada senza voltarsi" [made the smallest possible offer, and continued on his way without turning around] (p. 973). His journey does not permit even the briefest moment of compassion, either toward himself or toward others.

Finally, on the road to Camemi, the old man who is breaking stones under the midday sun points out the crows to him, the harbingers of death, as they fly overhead, again and again, croaking "against the ruthless sky." Even the landscape has an apocalyptic quality:

Brontolava ancora allontanandosi all'ambio della mula sotto il sole cocente: un sole che spaccava le pietre adesso, e faceva scoppiettare le stoppie quasi s'accendessero. Nel burrone, fra i due monti, sembrava d'entrare in una fornace; e il paese in cima al colle, arrampicato sui precipizi, disseminato fra rupi enormi, minato da caverne che lo lasciavano come sospeso in aria, nerastro, rugginoso, sembrava abbandonato, senza un'ombra, con tutte le finestre spalancate nell'afa, simili a tanti buchi neri, le croci dei campanili vacillanti nel cielo caliginoso.

[Still grumbling, as he ambled off at the mule's pace under the burning sun—a sun that splits rocks now, and made the stubble pop as if it were on fire. In the ravine, between the two mountains, it felt like a furnace; and the town on top of the hill, perched above the precipices, scattered among enormous cliffs, undermined by caverns that left it as if hanging in the air, blackish, rusty, seemed abandoned, without a shadow, with all the windows thrown open wide in the haze, like so many black holes, and the crosses on the bell towers swaying against the misty sky.] (p. 970)

The inorganic element triumphs. Life seems to have abandoned this barren landscape where only rocks and cliffs remain. The colors are those associated with hell: the blazing red color of the sun, and black. The protagonist moves in the void of a desolate land abandoned by humans: even the village seems abandoned. The only other allusion to human reality is to a blast furnace, an infernal mode of production—flames and scorching heat—with which Gesualdo is particularly familiar, having worked there as a boy. The prevalence of the inorganic element—the desert, the blast furnace, and later, the crows—are all apocalyptic images of a demonic universe, from which the image of the devil springs forth naturally, only to be reinforced immediately afterward by the presence of the old man. With this description Verga returns to the pivotal theme of the barren landscape previously outlined in *Rosso Malpelo*, whose universe is also predominantly constituted by mineral substances, by infertile sand, by peaks and gorges where no cricket "chirps" or bird "sings."

The empty space in *Vita dei campi* was subterranean. Instead, in *Mastro*, the void is evoked by images of precipices and overhanging caverns, which give us the impression that the village is "suspended in air," not resting on anything. The windows of the houses signify absence; they are "black holes," while the adjective "rusty" and the past participle "endangered" ("minato da caverne . . . nerastro, rugginoso" [endangered by caverns . . . blackish, rusty] {p. 970}) suggest the notion of a slow implacable corrosion. In such a landscape, everything seems precarious, crumbling, unstable: even the bell towers look as if they are "swaying." The final image of the crosses against the misty sky leaves us with yet another emblem of emptiness and death. If on the one hand the links—blast furnace/hell; fatigue/death; internal void/external void—symbolically underline Gesualdo's existential condition, on the other hand they allegorically allude to humanity's essential estrangement from destiny, as well as to the dissonance between the human condition and a nature that is scarred by the forces of both production and decay. The world of harmonious *correspondences* between the soul and the landscape, which could still unfold before Mena or (in the last part of *I Malavoglia*) before 'Ntoni, now no longer exists.

Equally apocalyptic and inorganic is the landscape Gesualdo has to cross to go from Vizzini to Camemi through the Petrajo gorge (even the place-name evokes the idea of harshness). Here the imagery recalls the allegories of the Baroque (so dear to Benjamin), which obsessively revolve around the figures of the skeleton and the corpse. The image of death is effectively evoked not only by the rotting carcass in the ditch, but also by the crows that, time and again, fly overhead croaking in the sky, against the "bare, parched, rocky" hills. Everywhere dust dominates. The prickly pear trees are "dusty"; "white with dust" are the shins of the old stone-cutter, whose eyes burn in the "dust." Immediately thereafter, Gesualdo's face becomes "white with dust" and the old man—and here the parallel is certainly not casual—also has "a dusty face." Finally the "faccia accesa e riarsa, bianca di polvere" [the parched and flushed face, white with dust] (p. 974) of the man is also described, evoking once more the image of barenness and death. The reminiscence of the biblical *pulvis* is linked to the image of the skeleton which can be perceived in the specular images of the old man and Gesualdo; in the "shins" and "fleshless arms" of the former, and in the "viso che pareva una maschera" [face which looked like a mask] (p. 974) of the latter. The scene that had opened with the description of the men sleeping in the ditch (the ditch with the carcass in it) as though they were corpses ("li trovò tutti quanti sdraiati bocconi nel fossato, di qua e di là, col viso coperto di mosche, e le braccia stese" [he found them all lying on their stomachs in the ditch, here and there, their faces covered with flies and their arms stretched out] {p. 974}) ends consistently with the old man raising his eyes to follow the crows' flight "quasi sapesse cosa volevano e li aspettasse" [as if he knew what they wanted and was waiting for them] (p. 975).

Gesualdo's race against time becomes a race toward death. The complete transformation of time-as-life into time-as-work desiccates existence, reducing it to an empty skeleton. The attempt to dominate the irrational—the reality of feelings and impulses—by placing it under the tyrannical control of economic logic is possible only at the expense of an inner devastation, which not only takes the form of self-destruction but also leaves Gesualdo, even in the first part of the novel, with a sense of guilt and loneliness.

Nature undergoes a similar transformation. It is either an obstacle to be overcome, or it takes on the appearance of an agricultural landscape, of cultivated nature, which is therefore the result of productive labor. Gesualdo's satisfaction at the sight of his Canziria property confirms this transformation. The moon, with its "dawn-like glimmer" illuminates his property, the sheaves piled up and the oxen crouched around the yard, while the wind carries the sound of the bells worn by the beasts of burden and the "stormire delle messi ancora in piedi" [rustling of the uncut wheat] (p. 977). Gesualdo utilizes all his senses. He looks around, perceives distant sounds, and senses the odors ("odore dei covoni nell'aia" [scent of the sheaves in the yard] {p. 976}). But his sight, his hearing, and his sense of smell do not establish a symbiotic relationship with nature nor are they endowed with sensual synesthesia, as is the case in the symbolist tradition. Landscape is above all the landscape of property.

The last part of chapter 5 introduces for a moment an idyllic world that acquires greater significance because it follows immediately upon Gesualdo's feverish activity to settle his business matters. It is here that we see how property (land) can become a last refuge for a social class that is still capable of maintaining a direct relationship with the land. Gesualdo reflects a stage in the economic development of the new bourgeoisie, a stage in which it was still possible to pause for a moment and reestablish contact with nature through its rural landscape. Time stands still long enough to engender memories and tenderness and to thrust Gesualdo into an existential dimension. As his memories unfold, it seems as if his career as a social climber can take on an epic rhythm that endows it with meaning and value. The long interior monologue that recalls his social ascent from laborer to businessman and landowner slowly winds its way through reiterations and repetition, through noun and verbal phrases, until it finally reaches a climax. But the epic moment belongs only to the past. The chronotope undergoes a momentary transformation, enabling us to perceive a different temporal and spatial dimension, but immediately after this, its usual coordinates are reestablished. The rigid rule that excludes the possibility of a respite in the modern world is confirmed, the idyll is at once contradicted and rudely denied. After having proudly declared to Diodata—"E la mia roba? ... me l'hanno data i genitori forse? Non mi son fatto da me quel che sono?" [And my property? ... Did I by any chance get it from my parents? Didn't I make myself what I am?] (p. 981)—Gesualdo is obliged, at the sight of the woman's tears, to come to terms with the dark side of his social ascent: "Che vuoi? Non si può far sempre quel che si desidera. Non sono piú padrone ... come quando ero un povero diavolo senza nulla" [That's the way it goes! You can't always do what you want to. I'm no longer master ... as when I was a poor devil with nothing] (p. 981). Paradoxically, as a landowner he is denied the possibility of being master of his own time and destiny; he is alienated from himself, condemned to a "terrible fate." If in *I Malavoglia* the contrast between values and feelings on the one hand and economic interests and cynicism on the other is narratively developed in the contrasts between the villagers of Trezza and the Toscano family, in *Mastro* the conflict has been interiorized, it all takes place within the protagonist, tormenting him like a "wasp." Gesualdo's furious screams bring the respite to an abrupt end, and the last part of the chapter acquires once again the frantic rhythm of the previous pages. Canziria is not Gesualdo's homeland, nor is it the destination of his journey. It is only a casual stage. In fact, in the chapter that follows, the feverish journey toward Fiumegrande is continued with a race against the storm.

Gesualdo's last journey takes him from the country to the city, from a rural landscape—which is also the landscape of property and production—to the duke's palace in Palermo, where the scenery is one of sloth and emptiness, of useless liveries and carriages. In Gesualdo's eyes, the city symbolizes unproductive squandering and parasitic activity. This stance reflects Verga's ideological parameters, which he took from Franchetti and Sonnino and the supporters of the "agricultural alternative."[3] From the vantage point of the guest house, Gesualdo can see beneath him the life in the palace, with its senseless waste, its empty pomp and ceremony, and the servants' idleness. And so the property that Gesualdo has accumulated so laboriously is completely squandered. Ironically, the Dantean law of the *contrappasso* is working against him while he is still alive.

His condition, starting with his departure from Vizzini, seems to be already reversed. From being active it has become passive; from a subject capable of influencing the people around him, Gesualdo has now become a target of their aims and ambitions. He no longer has a dynamic relationship with the landscape, nor does he have the courage to face it; from his litter, he can only see it "pass by": "Appena don Gesualdo fu in istato di poter viaggiare, lo misero in lettiga e partirono per la città. Era una giornata piovosa. Le case note, dei visi di conoscenti che si voltavano appena, sfilavano attraverso gli sportelli della lettiga"

[As soon as don Gesualdo was fit to travel, they put him in a litter and set off for the city. It was raining. Familiar houses, and faces of acquaintances who scarcely turned around, passed by the windows of the litter] (p. 1170).

He is leaving friends behind him in the village: Diodata, who has come on purpose to say goodbye, as well as the faithful Nardo, who accompanies him to the outskirts of Vizzini. Diodata and Nardo represent the last link with the rural and patriarchal universe from which Gesualdo estranged himself in order to pursue the logic of economic interest.

Gesualdo's farewell to Vizzini reminds us of 'Ntoni's departure from Trezza, although it is less lyrical and more cruel. Gesualdo is not consoled by the glitter of the friendly constellations nor by the familiar rumble of the sea. Instead, he is accompanied by two characters who fill him only with remorse. From the window of his litter, he tries in vain to catch a glimpse of Diodata and his natural children, to whom he could not and will not be able to leave even the tiniest portion of his property. When he puts his hand in his pocket to give a few coins to Nardo, who is faithful to the very last, Gesualdo realizes he has nothing to give. Hence, the logic of property takes vengeance on the very person who has followed its rules so consistently. He who has sacrificed everything to accumulate wealth now does not even have a coin to satisfy a generous impulse. Impotence and passivity are reflected in the images of decay that accompany Gesualdo's litter. The mud on the country road, "il campanile perduto nella nebbia" [the bell tower lost in the fog] (p. 1171), "i fichi d'India rigati dalla pioggia" [the prickly pears streaked by the rain] (p. 1171), all are further emblems of death. If in *I Malavoglia* another world was possible, if only one of exile and vagabondage, in *Mastro* Gesualdo's last journey leads to nothingness.

Even in the last part of *I Malavoglia*, one of the protagonists is led toward death. It is Master 'Ntoni who, in Alfio Mosca's cart, is taken to the town hospital. But this parallel should not be unduly emphasized. In *I Malavoglia,* death is not a private matter. Instead, it is woven into ethnological time, which governs the collective psyche. The whole family, in fact, goes through the experience of death, with solidarity, not only with the death of Bastianazzo and Longa but even with Master 'Ntoni who, however, dies alone in hospital. Contrary to this, *Mastro* leads us into the modern world where time is historical and the inner and individual life is removed from the community. Death cannot be placed within a dimension of continuing time, as is instead the case with Master 'Ntoni (when Master 'Ntoni dies, Alessi follows the path that he has traced; he buys back the house by the medlar tree). In *Mastro* death takes on the meaning of total obliteration or, as Bakhtin puts it, of a "complete end." It is an individual death, a death that annihilates any sense of personal accomplishment and leads to nothingness.

Verga's pessimism thus forms a perfect circle. If it is impossible to exist within the boundaries of the eternal recurrence typical of the archaic-rural civilization undermined by "progress," it is even more impossible to live within the purely economic boundaries of the modern world. To step into a modern world is to set out on a road where no return, no redemption, and no inner development are possible. It involves undertaking a journey that is not a true journey—that is to say, a passage from one point to another, or the pursuit and discovery of a destination endowed with meaning. If in *I Malavoglia* the journey is impossible, in *Mastro-don Gesualdo,* it is senseless. Upon close scrutiny, in fact, we can see how this novel is not about individual assertion and social climbing, but rather about the absurdity of such aspirations. The liberal myth of the self-made man is turned inside out. Even the novel dealing with "trials and tribulations," which by then should have replaced the "idyllic" novel, is dissolved from within. What meaning can we possibly attribute to the personal trials that are to be overcome in the absurd pursuit of success, which rewards its victors with the most tragic of defeats? *Mastro* has only the outward appearance of the traditional novel whose parabolic structure is marked first by the rise and then by the decline of an individual's life. In reality, Gesualdo carries death within him right from the very start. What accompanies him incessantly is the very void that follows his every movement even at the moment of his greatest triumphs. Although many novels end with the death of the protagonist, in very few do we see death portrayed with such devastating force. Even the cancer, which is slowly consuming Gesualdo, becomes, in his eyes a metaphor of property: the inevitable outcome of all the angst brought about by the logic of economic interests. But can a journey whose relentless outcome is death, a journey that is accompanied by death and whose destination is death, can this really be called a journey in which a man looks toward a future with an opening up of horizons and perspectives, having meaning and purpose?[4] Gesualdo's feverish life does not follow a straight trajectory. It wanders aimlessly and senselessly, until death finally brings him to rest. Verga dissolves, along with Defoe, the myth of the journey, which had contributed to the emergence of the bourgeois novel. With Verga the journey turns out to be merely an illusion. In reality, life does not follow any one direction in particular, it has neither a point of departure nor a point of arrival; it emerges from nothingness and returns to and fades into nothingness. It parades before our very eyes like those prickly pears spoiled by the rain. If we accept the conclusion that any attempt to direct life toward a destination is only an illusion, then its most authentic image is not the journey, but rather vagabondage.

THE JOURNEY IN IPPOLITO NIEVO'S NARRATIVE: TYPOLOGIES

Marinella Colummi Camerino

There are authors in nineteenth-century Italy who consciously exclude from their horizons the experience of open space and confine their adventures to the darkness of their imagination. Leopardi is an excellent example of a stationary traveler.[1] His journeys are predominantly imaginary journeys. If not, the journey becomes pure escape, as in the case of *Dialogo della Natura e di un Islandese* where the author longs for new places and atmospheres.

There are writers who, instead, nourish their quest through real journeys. Ippolito Nievo is one of these itinerant travelers. His journeys are physical before being imaginary experiences; they are spatial before becoming imagined. Nievo's entire life seems to be defined by an eighteenth-century paradigm: to wander in order to acquire self-knowledge. His demonstrated social activism serves to exorcise not only the inactivity of the "decade of preparation," but also, on a more personal level as he indicated in many letters, the idleness of his personal time. His life is also characterized by a propensity for disguise to both conceal his true self and at the same time augment the sensation of existence.[2] The disconcerting number of experiences he accumulated in his lifetime reveals an almost excessive thirst for participation, which would suggest the desire to compensate for a sense of inadequacy. In the *Novelliere campagnuolo* or in the collection of short stories Nievo wanted to publish under this title, the journey defines and semiotically structures a complex reality. The journey is an event, but it is also a notion pregnant with images, perceptions, and volitions.[3] As a rule, it constitutes a physical link between two diverse and removed worlds: the bourgeois and the rural. By linking and comparing these two worlds the journey redefines the boundaries not only of reality but especially of literary reality. In so doing Ippolito Nievo's *Novelliere campagnuolo* represents the most comprehensive attempt, in mid-nineteenth-century Italy, to confer literary status on the rural, archaic world of his time.

In this work the journey is structured in two opposite ways, which only on the surface may seem complementary: a bourgeois traveler goes to the country and a peasant journeys to the city. Everything begins in *La Nostra famiglia di campagna* with a pleasant journey on a cart. From the outset, the mode of transportation recalls a "low" literary tradition and foreshadows the parodistic reduction to which the adventure of the heroes is destined. The traveler, accompanied by a friend who is "sollazzevole e disposto con mente . . . serena alla vita" [cheerful with a serene . . . attitude toward life], wanders through the Mantua countryside. The soft and rolling hills of the landscape around Solferino are perfect agents for the contemplation and the enjoyment of the picturesque in nature through the recollection of poetic memories:

> "Cosí scendevamo a trotto prudentissimo dai colli di Solferino, riandando fra noi le piccole avventure occorseci, e le bellezze del lago di Garda e la festa de' suoi giardini, e il pittoresco incurvarsi delle sponde, e l'azzurro dell'acqua, e il superbo promontorio di Sirmione . . . e le poetiche memorie di Catullo e di Pindemonte spigolate lí intorno."
>
> [So we came, at a prudent trot, down from the hills of Solferino, going back over the little adventures that had happened to us, and the charms of Lake Garda, and the glory of its gardens, and the picturesque curving of the shores, and the blue of the water, and the superb Sirmione

V. Cabianca. *Ritorno dai campi* (Return from the fields). 1862. 75 x 151 cm. Alvaro Angiolini Collection, Livorno, Italy.

promontory . . . and the poetic memories of Catullus and Pindemonte gleaned from thereabouts.]⁴

Suddenly, this idyllic voyage is interrupted: the cart loses a wheel and the passengers fall to the ground. The overturning of the vehicle parodistically depicts the reversal of a code and signals the beginning of a different type of journey. The aesthetic pleasure derived from the physical surroundings is now replaced by knowledge, and the picturesque qualities of nature are substituted with a countryside cultivated by manual labor.

The journey, according to eighteenth-century tradition, becomes a paradigm of experience and didactic conventions. It has been said wrongly that in this short story Nievo utilizes the formula of the journey as an artificial structure in order to link together the different encounters with country folks and to illustrate the reality of peasant life. What is true instead is that Nievo employs the traditional structure and adapts it to his requirements without ever reducing it to a purely illustrative function. For Nievo the journey becomes the literary topos where the physical and the imaginary voyages coincide—a paradigm of the difficult path that leads not only to self-awareness but also to the demonstration of the goodness possessed by the peasant classes: "Voglio rappresentarti, o ingenuo lettore per ischizzi e profili quella parte piú pura dell'umana famiglia che vive nei campi . . . innamorarti di coloro che allenano per te e de' quali in onta al diuturno consorzio conosci ben poco indole, mente, e costumi" [I want to show you, simple reader, by sketches and outlines that purest part of the human family that works the land . . . to make you love those who labor for you and about whose character, thinking, and customs you know very little].⁵ If Nievo's stated goal is to augment the knowledge society has of the rural masses and to reveal the true nature of the peasant classes, the path he has chosen to achieve this becomes tortuous and uneven. First, the subject matter is by definition "viva e bollente" [hot and lively].⁶ Second, and more important, the task is made more arduous by the readers who, like the quarrelsome traveling companion, show reluctance in accepting the proposition that the traveler has the burden of proof.

The journey is therefore a sustained metaphoric argument through which an indifferent and hostile bourgeoisie will be slowly but surely persuaded. It is also the wandering and capricious path of a narration that legitimatizes common discourse, "trattenimenti di ciarle" [idle gossip] or "dialogo di confidenza" [informal conversation], by utilizing a variety of registers that range from the ironic to the aggressive to the didactic:

> Bisogna che tu pigli in santa pace questa mia maniera di scrivere, o amico lettore: giacché non per nulla ad un trattenimento di ciarle meglio che ad una lettura ti invitai fin da principio; e cosí come in un dialogo di confidenza io n'andrò via svolazzando di palo in frasca, persuaso che tu bonariamente terrai dietro al filo di seta dove ho costretta la gamba.
>
> [You need to peacefully accept this style of mine, dear reader: since I invited you from the beginning to an idle gossip rather than to a reading; so that in this informal conversation, I shall be jumping from one thing to another, safe in the knowledge that you will good-naturedly hold on to the silk thread with which I pull your leg.][7]

The encounters of the itinerant journeymen—be they imaginary or real—are symmetrically arranged on the one hand to highlight the qualities and values of the rural world and on the other hand to emphasize the negative aspects of bourgeois society. If the encounters with the urban situations and characters are presented as typical, the encounters with the rural world are governed by a logic that is highly idealized. Given the exceptional qualities possessed by Nievo's characters, they are positioned outside or almost outside the bounds of history like "certe piante tropicali sorprese nelle terre polari nel raffreddamento terrestre" [that] "rimasero né morte né vive, esseri d'altro tempo, d'altro clima estranei affatto alla vicenda de' mondiali movimenti" [certain tropical plants caught in the arctic during the ice ages, which remained neither alive nor dead, like beings from another time, another climate, entirely unaffected by the events of world history]. The peasant who first notices the travelers, fallen from the cart, describes to them the historical context of a land that not only "dà assai lavoro e poco poco da mangiare" [requires a lot of work and produces very little to eat] but is also a source of exploitation and disease. But from the high and dignified forehead of the old peasant one can sense the aura of an ancient past filled with "operosa e libera convivenza" [industrious and free partnership] of someone who does not know and does not wish to know the alienation associated with and caused by modern economic forces.[8]

The projection into the past, at a time when the values of the present are being mercilessly swept away, underlines the precariousness of ideals. The bearers of these ideals are themselves the survivors of a lost world, and as a result they are placed outside history. Real and metaphoric, the estrangement of the rural world is not only an exile to be conquered, it also represents Nievo's dramatic invitation to bring back the memories of a vanished past. It is on the vision of a world that has been overtaken, and on the necessity to recall it, that the true meaning of Nievo's idyllic universe rests; not, as has been said in the past, on a return to the ideals of purity and diversity that the country represents.[9]

The journey from the rural world, which is systematically described as remote, hidden, and not easily accessible, toward the city and history can only be characterized as traumatic.[10] Contrary to the free and conscious journeys undertaken by the middle class, the peasant journeyman does not wish to leave his rural nest. The journey for him becomes a negative experience, and the mobility associated with the voyage leads to social displacement.

Whether set in a domestic story, *Santa di Arra*, or in a brief heroic-comic epic, *Milione del bifolco*, or even in a pathetic-sentimental adventure, *Conte di Pecoraio*, the journey does not change the protagonist who undertakes it. Instead, given its alienating nature, the journey serves to reconfirm the peasant's original identity by leading him or her back to the "place" to which he or she is physically linked: a place in which the predictability of individual and collective destinies is guaranteed by its spatial paradigms. The departure from the village is a departure from one's self. As Santa journeys to Brescia by train to search for a cholera-stricken brother, she is shocked and disoriented by the invisible power of the locomotive: "Quegli alberi, quelle case che parevano cadere all'indietro per la veemenza della corsa le davano il capogiro . . . insomma era cosí sorpresa che a nulla poteva pensare come si trovasse fuori affatto dalla vita" [Those trees, those houses, which seemed to fall away behind the speeding train, made her dizzy, . . . in fact she was so surprised that she could not think of anything, as if she were not a part of life at all].[11] The train—in one of the first references to it in Italian literature—is the agent that shocks, causes bewilderment, and derails the character's spatial-temporal perceptions. Maria, the protagonist of *Conte Pecoraio*, is another example of the process of estrangement. From the time she leaves her native village on foot without anyone's knowledge, she finds herself in a progressive path of self-destruction that leads her to assume a false identity and to the tragic loss of her child.

In these journeys the city is the source of destructive forces, which assail, tempt, and weaken the protagonist's integrity. Within the walls of the city, Santa falls prey to cholera, and Carlone will be deceived, ridiculed, and mistreated.[12] And like Renzo Tramaglino in *I promessi sposi*, Carlone will not learn anything from his experiences—only what he must not become.

In the rural milieu the journey is circular. If its beginning threatens the serenity of an idyllic existence, its completion reestablishes the original state. The peasant protagonists who venture into evil by undertaking journeys reemerge, at their completion, much more grounded in self-identity. The return has an ethical dimension. It is the recognition of the "place" that shapes our character and to which we are viscerally tied.

Ippolito Nievo makes use of the classical typology of the journey as a return home in order to depict the rural world as a world where life's events are shaped by the physical milieu that generates them.

The short story *Il Varmo*, represents an important departure from the classical typology of the journey. Traditionally this short story has been seen to be much closer ideologically to the *Confessioni* than to the collection of which it is an integral part. *Il Varmo* is also considered unique because, in its representation of the rural world, the author not only foreshadows characters and situations that will appear in the *Confessioni*, but also because in it Nievo creates a new and original spatial-temporal dynamic not present in the earlier short stories.

The journey is once again a spatial experience. The narrator imagines a traveling "artist" who is able to reach remote places not normally known to the ordinary traveler who suffers "col mal del quattrino nel fegato" [with money sickness in his heart]. Even in this short story, therefore, the idyllic moment is linked to a physical place no mattter how remote and circuitous the path to reach it might be. But the Friuli countryside quickly reveals to the traveler new and different characteristics never encountered before. These new characteristics are unveiled from the opening dedication, "immagini apprese dall'anima in un'ora di pace . . . moltiplicate dal sentimento pòpolano di vaghi fantasmi il sacrario del cuore" [images captured by the soul in an hour of peace, . . . multiplied by the mind, populate the sanctuary of the heart with shapeless ghosts].[13] The frequent use of adjectives of endearment and the affective mode of expression soon transform the countryside into a personal myth. The journey becomes a pretext for recollection. The physical remoteness of the spot blends into the temporal remoteness of the lost childhood. As a result the idyllic is connected to childhood; in fact, it is childhood. Spatial distance, which may have been viewed as a strong component in the preceding short stories, highlights the difference between the ideal and the real, between the idyllic and the historical, and it acquires a temporal dimension that resolves these juxtapositions into a harmonious reality. This same distance will also, on a diagetic plane, eliminate life's implicit contradictions.

During childhood, the transfiguration of reality can be total and complete; time can stand still, and human existence can blend with nature. The free and innocently sensual games of Favitta and Sgricciolo in the "bel luogo" [beautiful place] bring to mind "bel endroit" [beautiful place] of Georges Sand and Rousseau's "lieu si cheri" [place so dear]. But childhood with its idyllic dimension soon converges into adolescence and maturity. It seems strange that critics, especially those who search for stylistic elegance, have examined the parts of the short story that deal with the idyllic aspect of childhood and have generally ignored its conclusion. The ending becomes important and necessary when viewed in the context of a narrative dynamic preoccupied not only with the idyllic moments but also with the process through which these moments become threatened and conquered by history. The events of adolescence and the "dolce amaro" [bittersweet][14] wedding between Sgricciolo and Favitta—by now another man's widow—reveal how easily the idyllic refuge of childhood can be disintegrated. From the point of view of the "history" of the protagonists, in fact, it is impossible to go back. As the milieu of one's individual and social history, the idyllic moment will never again be accessible. The physical accessibility, so prevalent in the *Novelliere,* will be replaced in the *Confessioni* by the power of recollection. The physical journey to the childhood milieu will only be approximated by longing glances backward where absence replaces presence.

In the *Confessioni,* therefore, the meaning and the structure of the journey are completely altered. Having integrated the "country" into the flow of history—demonstrated by the ridiculous revolution of Portogruaro where the peasants and the city dwellers are, together, the negative protagonists—Nievo's bourgeois traveler has no "elsewhere" to go to. He follows an open quest guided only by events of history. The journey becomes, according to the metaphor used by the octogenarian narrator, the "journey of life," divided into stages, which progress from "la prima infanzia al cominciar della vecchiaia" [from early infancy to the beginning of old age] through the "combattuta giovinezza" [struggling youth] to the "stanchissima virilità" [exhausted virility].[15]

In the *Confessioni,* the journey is developed according to a regular rhythm, determined by the protagonist's biological framework and by his spatial autonomy. Space (as Bakhtin states) is an important organizing center in the temporal progression of the narration. From Fratta to Portogruaro, from Venice to Europe and to America, the narrative shifts the plot away from the horizon of fulfilled experiences. There is, in Nievo's strong emphasis on the biological determinism of space, a certain anxiety for completeness and conclusions.[16]

It has been said that Carlo Altoviti's journey becomes a sort of personal challenge and a progressive quest for the acquisition of experiences and status.[17] Many of the same critics have also suggested that, although this interpretation is frequently given to the first part of the *Confessioni,* it becomes more problematic when considering the rest of the work. In fact, if one can utilize this interpretative framework, one must openly state that as far as a bildungsroman goes, this novel does not follow the classical closed model very faithfully. The path that leads to Carlino's personal development is, contrary to the classical model, irregular, circuitous, and as uneven as is the narrative that reveals it.[18] But the very unevenness, which critics have often singled out as a deficient element, allows Nievo to capture the profound meaning of a paradoxical reality to which his octogenarian narrator tries to give temporary form:

> Io non sono né teologo né sapiente né filosofo; pure voglio sputare la mia sentenza, come il viaggiatore che per quanto ignorante, può a buon diritto giudicare se il paese da lui percorso sia povero o ricco, spiacevole o bello. Ho vissuto ottantatré anni, figliuoli, posso dunque dire la mia.

[I am neither theologian, nor sage, nor philosopher; still, I want to come up with my verdict, like the traveler who, however ignorant, has a perfect right to judge whether the country he is traveling through is poor or rich, unpleasant or beautiful. I have been alive for eighty-three years, my children, so I can surely have my say.][19]

The old man's sententious speech stems from the fact that he has reached the end of his life. His words may be seen more as a form of compensation than as a means of revealing life's precarious nature. The journey discloses its purpose when it is completed. In fact, Carlino has been an "ignorant" traveler not only because of his modest culture, but because life has been to him "quasi inesplicabile" [almost unexplainable], as he himself states.[20] After the stages of childhood and early adolescence (for the description of which Nievo employs an archaic stylistic approach), the increasing contact with the forces of historical events causes in Carlino a progressive blindness, which makes him unable to see and interpret the world. It would require too many examples to demonstrate that in crucial moments Carlino does not understand, does not see, or ignores, what is happening to him. Here are a few instances from chapter 11, when the protagonist is made a member of the Grand Council and later on becomes, after the fall of the Republic, secretary of the newly established municipality:

> Mio padre era proprio tornato di Turchia a tempo, per far me poverello partecipe senza saperlo di tali codarde castronerie. E d'altra parte cosa valeva il sapere? . . . Il maggior malanno si era che ci intendeva ben poco . . . Io era certo quello che ci capiva meno . . . Alle volte mi guardava indietro sorprendendomi di esser arrivato fin là, e non comprendendo né il perché né il come; ma la corrente mi trascinava. . . . Io girai alcuni anni lo spiedo, fui studente e un po' anche cospiratore: indi tranquillo cancelliere, pio patrizio veneto nel Maggior Consiglio e segretario della Municipalità: da amante spensierato di tutto mi mutai di colpo in soldato: di soldato in ozioso un'altra volta, poi in intendente e in

maggiordomo: finii a maritarmi e a sonar l'organo. In questo perpetuo su e giù, se salii o scesi lo direte voi.

[My father had come back just in time from Turkey to involve poor ignorant me in such cowardly nonsense. And on the other hand, what good did it do to know? . . . The greatest misfortune about it was that he understood very little of the situation. . . . I was certainly the one who understood the least. . . . Sometimes I looked behind, surprised that I had come so far and not understanding either why or how, but the current pulled me along. . . . For several years I tried my hand at different things, I was a student— and then also a bit of a conspirator, then contented chancellor, then pious patrician in the Venetian Grand Council and secretary of the municipality: from carefree lover all of a sudden I changed into a soldier: from soldier again into a loafer, then into a superintendent and into a butler: I ended up by getting married and playing the organ. In all this perpetual up and down, you tell me if I was going up or going down.][21]

These episodes do not constitute a history of acquired personal knowledge, nor are they a narration of progressive and consistent experiences. Carlino's metamorphoses are presented as casual stages in the exploration of the world that is neither desired nor always logical, but often interrupted. Others will assume the responsibility to establish some semblance of order in these varied episodes.

Carlino explains the continuous fluctuations in his life with the absence of a unified people and a nation to which the individual can conform. The octogenarian aphoristically states: "la vita dell'individuo non può misurare la vita delle nazioni" [the life of the individual cannot be a measure of the life of nations].[22] If man's subjective destiny cannot be interpreted or measured against that of nations, this means there is no identification between public and private spheres, that personal feelings clash with civic virtues, that there is no affinity between ideals and real, personal, economic interests.[23] Since the day of his departure from the archaic world of Fratta, Carlino has had ample opportunity to observe these phenomena.

But is it possible for a journey constituted of heterogeneous stages to fulfill and prove the archetypical metaphor of the bildungsroman? I think it can, even in an age of modernity not easily receptive to synthesis. We shall be able to do so, first, if we accept a compromise, and second, if we see maturity not as a definitive and finite goal but rather as the attainment of a precarious and unstable plateau. The compromise is to be discovered not in the actions but in the personality of the protagonist. As many critics have stated, Carlino is a modest hero who lacks the strength to avoid being involved in or swept up by the events that confront him. If society's collective destiny does not correspond to that of the members who constitute it, the only thing left for the individual to do is to conform to the public will. This is the price to be paid in the modern process of socialization. Carlino is the only character who is both capable enough and willing to do so. In this sense he is the only truly modern character of the *Confessioni*.

Carlino is a protagonist who consciously engages in recollection. Memory crystallizes the present so as to allow us to live and understand its precariousness.[24] Memory for Carlino is escape and salvation, destruction and conquest, torment and solace. To remember means to be able to stop the flux of time; to capture images and events like a collector who gathers objects in his personal museum only to rearrange them in order to recognize them.[25]

Many times in the course of his life Carlino goes back to Fratta, and each time he returns, he recalls his most remote past. The journey backward is both real and imaginary. In one of his visits, while the Pisana remains on the outside without memories or preoccupations, Carlino loses himself in the halls of the castle (a metaphor for the past).[26] Much has been written on the meaning of the return to the past in the *Confessioni*. Is it an escape into the past, or is it an active recovery of what was? Although the majority of critics now tends to accept the latter, the problem can best be analyzed if one looks at the way the return to the past is structured. Often the journey backward in time becomes part of and is parallel to the journey backward in space.[27] The repetition of the journey's path reveals the changeability of the subject who undertakes it. Carlino, during his many returns, is always the same and always different. The spatial experience defines subjective time. The subject becomes aware of the historicity of being. In this identifiable process—in which sensation and memory create the true self-representation—lies the authentic historical dimension of the *Confessioni*. The return to a lost childhood is not therefore a return to salvation; instead, it is a return to an ontological source, which gives one direction in view of the precariousness of the journey.

But the journey is not complete. Carlino's biological life comes to an end as does his spatial mobility due to "lo scirocco degli ottanta anni nelle gambe" [the unsteadiness of my eighty years on my legs]. Yet, the antinomies that have characterized his life do not reach a heightened sense of awareness. Carlino is old but not mature.[28] Many trials still lie ahead. Youth, in the real and metaphorical sense, must still pass the test even if the real protagonists will now be his sons and grandchildren. In many ways the novel of the octogenarian is a novel of the youthful existence that refuses to die; of a fluid state that does not and cannot solidify. It suggests that in the modern world the journey may well be an open path.

TRAVEL AS INSPIRATION IN PASCOLI'S POETRY

V. R. Giustiniani

In Pascoli's time, few Italians (if any) were able to enjoy the pleasures of travel: perhaps only a handful of aristocrats carrying on the tradition of the Grand Tour inherited from the eighteenth century. For ordinary people, travel was dictated by economic necessity and was a source of painful experiences. Peasants and workers flocked to America to escape the misery and hardships of home. "Partire è un poco morire" [Leaving is a little like dying], the saying goes, and a great number of unfortunate people in crowded railway cars or on the upper decks of ocean-going immigrant steamers of that era had ample opportunity to ascertain how true it was. The middle classes had to conform to the policy of the newly established Kingdom of Italy (1861), aimed at integrating into a single nation the seven separate states that had been Italy. No other single measure seemed more apt to cement the political unity achieved at such a heavy cost, than to transfer civil servants, military personnel, and teachers of all levels from the North to the South and vice versa.

"Partire è un poco morire": this was the feeling of young Pascoli too, when he, as a newly appointed university teacher, had to leave his native Romagna (a region south of the Po delta) for Matera, a city in the deep and desolate South. But he had many more reasons for grieving than simple nostalgia: his father was murdered when he was still a child, and his mother died shortly thereafter, so he did not long for any newer or broader horizons than those of his own village. He was not a Ulysses "who saw the towns and knew the minds of many men."[1] He yearned instead for a calm shelter, a home, and a circle of loving people. He had turned his affections to his two sisters, Ida and Maria, who embodied his lost dream of family happiness. Both sisters joined him two years later, when he had the opportunity of coming back to Central Italy, after being transferred to Massa. Here he managed to rebuild, at least in part, the never forgotten family of his childhood. Maria remained with him until his death. She accompanied him when he started a new career as a university professor in Messina, and later when he transferred to Pisa. In Bologna, where he was closer to his native haunts, he crowned his academic and literary success by taking over the professorship that had been Carducci's.

Pascoli traveled within Italy only as much as was required by his job as teacher and by certain special tasks assigned to him by the Ministry of Education. He never left Italy. Yet it would not be an overstatement to say that travel is one of the most effectual sources of his poetry, if only because it was for him the cause of bitter experiences. Unlike Carducci, D'Annunzio, or even Dante, Pascoli never describes in detail the sites and landscapes he visited, choosing instead to depict them by means of allusions. Images of travel are captured by Pascoli in their most significant resonance only when they signify torment or despair: the day in which one has said "ai dolci amici addio" [farewell to dear friends].[2] Thus travel—whatever the route taken and places visited—is tantamount to disrupting the natural flow of life. Even returning home is not always a joy, nor is it a reward for the pain and effort expended. Very often it means disillusion instead, when one compares the present reality to the image of home held during the long years of absence. In this manner, the return brings about an awareness that every endeavor to fulfill a wish or dream is useless, that "we . . . pine for what is not."[3]

A few examples from Pascoli's poetry will serve to illustrate more fully his treatment of the theme of travel. We shall limit our examination to only four of his more representative poems.

In "L'isola dei poeti," Sicily reveals herself to the traveler approaching the Straits of Messina by train as a snow-white mountain (Mount Etna) against a rosy cloud and a blue sky. This vision of the island seen from afar is not atypical or unusual: it is a sort of painting where colors prevail over lines. Subsequently, the landscape fades into an image of ancient pastoral poetry leaving the reader suspended in doubt as to whether Pascoli is really seeing or dreaming:

> Il treno andava. Gli occhi a me la brezza
> pungea tra quella ignota ombra lontana;
> e m'invadea le vene la dolcezza
>   antelucana:
> . . . .
> Quel crocitare mi destò. Di fronte
> m'eri, o Sicilia, o nuvola di rosa
> sorta dal mare! E nell'azzurro un monte:
>   l'Etna nevosa.
> Salve, o Sicilia! Ogni aura che qui muove,
> pulsa una cetra od empie una zampogna,
> e canta e passa . . . Io era giunto dove
>   giunge chi sogna.
>
> [The train was moving. My eyes were burning
> with the fresh wind blowing
> from that unknown and distant darkness;
> and my veins filled with the sweetness
>   of that southern land:
> . . . .
> The hovering of the crows awakened me, and there
> you were in front of me, oh Sicily, oh rosy cloud
> risen from the sea! And in the blue a mountain:
>   snow-covered Etna
> Hail, oh Sicily! Every gentle breeze that moves here
> plays upon a lyre or fills a bagpipe
> and sings and passes on . . . . I had arrived where
>   dreamers arrive.][4]

The poem consists of fourteen sapphic strophes, but only one of these (the second one quoted above) deals concretely with Sicily. At the end, Sicily becomes a landscape peopled by the poets of yore, and Pascoli imagines himself to be one of them.

The contours of the landscape are even less evident when the poet, in the poem "Pietole," deals with an emigrant's vision of an unknown country where he hopes to find a better future:

> Ché nell'autunno è per lasciare i campi,
> il campagnolo, e dire addio per sempre
> alla sua verde Pietole. Ché fugge
> la Patria; dove, e' non lo sa per ora.
> . . . .
> Ora a quel vento c' cómpita cantando
> strane parole a chieder pane e fuoco,
> acqua e lavoro, oltr'alpi ed oltre mare,
> sotto altro sole . . .
>   —*Ich bin Italiener*
>   *Ich bin hungrig* . . .—.

> [Because in the autumn the peasant is about to
> leave the field, and say farewell forever
> to his green Pietole. Because he is fleeing
> his homeland; for where, he does not know for now
> . . . .
> It is now the duty of that wind
> to sing strange lyrics begging for bread and fire,
> water and work, beyond the Alps and beyond the sea,
> under a different sun . . .
>   —I am Italian
>   I am hungry . . .—.][5]

Pietole (formerly known as Andes), a village near Mantua, was Virgil's birthplace, and the reminiscence of the First Eclogue serves in "Pietole" as a scenario for the motif of the journey. Meliboeus too had to leave home: "nos patriae fines et dulcia linquimus arva" [the pleasant and refined language of our homeland]⁶ Virgil's words translated into Italian, "ché è per fuggir la patria," underscore the bitterness of the departure undertaken under the constraint of distress and misery. It is this despair, expressed again with the words "dove non sa per ora" and again "e' cómpita cantando / strane parole . . . —*Ich bin Italiener / Ich bin hungrig . . .—,*" that gives significance to the poem.

Impressive variations of the motif of the journey are to be found in two more poems dealing with Ulysses's legend, "Il ritorno" and "L'ultimo viaggio." In ancient mythology Ulysses is the traveler par excellence. His myth has proved more vital than that of any other hero in modern literature. His multifaceted character has inspired authors of all ages, from Dante to Joyce. For Dante, he is at the same time a sinner and a hero, a deceiver and an explorer, who obeys the supreme mandate of human nature, "all men naturally desire knowledge" as Aristotle says, and Cicero reiterates, "innatus est in nobis cognitionis amor et scientiae" [the desire to seek love and knowledge is innate in us].⁷ In Canto 26 of Dante's *Inferno*, we recall Ulysses's words to his shipmates:

> "considerate la vostra semenza:
> fatti non foste a viver come bruti,
> ma per seguir virtute e canoscenza."
>
> [consider your origins:
> you were not born to live like brutes,
> but to pursue virtue and knowledge.]⁸

For Joyce, the *Odyssey* is a point of reference for everyday life. Pascoli's Ulysses is not the same as Homer's; more specifically, his depiction conforms with Homer's only until the hero's arrival at Ithaca. Both in the *Odyssey* and in "Il ritorno" Ulysses is the mariner who has unceasingly roamed the oceans in search of the home he was prevented from regaining by Poseidon's wrath. Both in the *Odyssey* and in "Il ritorno," he sleeps when the Phaeacians land him with all his treasures on Ithaca's shore. When he awakens, he does not recognize his home island. In the *Odyssey* he does not recognize it because Athena has shrouded the landscape with a dense fog to keep his reentry secret. When he realizes where he is, Ulysses rejoices.[9] In "Il ritorno," instead, he does not rejoice when his plight at long last comes to an end. The reality that confronts him at this point conflicts with the home he longed for during his adventures. Ithaca looks poor, deserted, barren. All the places that had appeared so fascinating during his inexperienced youth now lack attraction. Ulysses can hardly believe the words of a girl (the Arethusa of his dreams), approaching to wash her clothes for her wedding in the nearby brook (another evident *contaminatio* with the Nausicaa episode in book 6 of the *Odyssey*).[10] Thus Pascoli bestows a different meaning on the ancient legend. Ulysses has become another person. Man has no certitude of his being. The motif of travel serves to express an existential problem: What is happiness? What are the wishes one strives to fulfill? On what basis can life rest?

> Io era, io era mutato!
> Tu, patria, sei come a quei giorni!
> Io sì, mio soave passato,
> ritorno; ma tu non ritorni. . . .
>
> [I had, I had changed!
> You, homeland, are as you were in those days!
> I indeed, my sweet past,
> Return; but you do not return. . . .][11]

Similar thoughts are expressed in "L'ultimo viaggio." Here Pascoli returns only in part to the traditional Ulysses motif. In the *Odyssey*, the spirit of the diviner Teiresias, when evoked by Ulysses from the underworld, predicts that the hero indeed will return to Ithaca, but not for long. The aged Ulysses must soon depart again; he must leave his wife and cherished home in order to offer to his enemy Poseidon a sacrifice that will reconcile him to the god.[12] Only then will he be able to enjoy the serenity he always longed for: death will come to him "far from the sea." Or is it "out of the sea"? The Greek expression *ex halós* can be understood both ways.[13] Pascoli chooses the second meaning of this expression and consequently develops a new interpretation of the Ulysses myth. Homer's Ulysses does not undertake a new journey after his return to Ithaca. Dante's Ulysses meets his death before returning. Pascoli resorts to another *contaminatio* and takes from Homer the motif of the return home and from Dante (who possibly took it from Ovid) the motif of Ulysses's ultimate journey.[14] But Pascoli's treatment of Ulysses's journey is not undertaken to "follow virtue and knowledge" but only to revisit the places "del suo patire dolce e remoto" [of his sweet and distant suffering], such as the island of Calypso.[15] Calypso's island was also for Ulysses a place of suffering: he sacrificed Calypso's offer of immortality for his nostalgia to return home. Was Calypso thereafter his secret love forever? It seems to have been so. But Ulysses dies before ever meeting her again. In fact, in Pascoli's "L'ultimo viaggio," Ulysses's lifeless body is washed on the shores of the island of Calypso. When Calypso notices it, she throws herself on his body and covers it with her magnificent hair:

> Nudo tornava chi rigò di pianto
> le vesti eterne che la dea gli dava;
> bianco e tremante nella morte ancora,
> chi l'immortale gioventú non volle.
>   Ed ella avvolse l'uomo nella nube
> dei suoi capelli; ed ululò sul flutto
> sterile, dove non l'udia nessuno:
>   —Non esser mai! non esser mai! piú nulla,
> ma meno morte, che non esser piú!—.

[Naked returned the one who had streaked with tears
the eternal garments the goddess had given him
white and still trembling in death
the one who did not want immortal youth.

> And she enshrouded the man in the cloud
> of her hair; and she wailed on the sterile
> wave, where nobody could hear her:
> —Oh to never be! Never be! More of nothing
> but less of death, than not to be anymore!—.][16]

This conclusion might suggest that Pascoli sought a sentimental end to the myth he evoked. Calypso reminds us of Carducci's Melisenda:

> La donna sul pallido amante
> chinossi, recandolo al seno,
> tre volte la bocca tremante
> col bacio d'amore baciò,
> e il sole dal cielo sereno
> calando ridente nell'onda
> l'effusa di lei chioma bionda
> sul morto poeta irraggiò.

> [The woman over her pale lover
> leaned, gathering him to her breast
> three times her quivering mouth
> gave the kiss of love,
> and the sun, from the tranquil sky
> laughingly falling into the waves,
> shone the fountain of her golden hair
> in rays upon the dead poet.][17]

But the meaning of Carducci's poem goes far beyond the evoking of romantic effects. It is complementary to the meaning of "Il ritorno" (with which it can be associated): the time and the places we really cherish are those of our sufferings, as Pascoli puts it in another short poem entitled "La mia sera":

> O stanco dolore, riposa!
> La nube nel giorno piú nera
> fu quella che vedo piú rosa
> nell'ultima sera.

[Oh tired suffering, take rest!
The darkest cloud of the day
was the one I saw the rosiest
in the late evening.]¹⁸

The whole of Pascoli's work still awaits an adequate assessment. The theme of travel seems to have been especially neglected. All attempts made until now have failed to appreciate Pascoli's unique contribution to the understanding of the human plight as exemplified through his treatment of the motif of the journey. He should be, I believe, in the company of Dante and Manzoni, who also offered a compelling vision of life and humanity.

NEW AND TRADITIONAL FORMS OF NINETEENTH-CENTURY TRAVEL LITERATURE

Elvio Guagnini

Travel literature in Italy is becoming of late less and less the exclusive domain of an elite. As recently as a few years ago, whenever the topic was raised, it seemed that a very private subject was being broached. The study of travel literature was either linked to purely technical fields (such as texts for geographical study, geographical discoveries, the history of scientific knowledge, and so on) or it was associated with a host of other disciplines equally specialized in nature.

The history of the past two centuries teaches us that specific investigations of travel literature have been carried out, mainly during periods of profound social change. It also demonstrates that the greatest emphasis devoted to these studies took place during periods characterized by the special attention placed on contacts between different groups both within and outside one's own national boundaries. The factors that formed the basis for such investigations may be found in the increasingly accentuated process of upheaval and transformation in society. They include geographical explorations and research in ethnology and anthropology; changing cultural and political relations; emigration; colonial expansion; the growth of tourism and new means of mass communication; the technological revolutions; and the exploration of space.

Italian scholarship has been marked by a particularly important period of reasearch during the late nineteenth and early twentieth centuries, mainly because of the impact of geographical and scientific discoveries. This period, characterized by the editing of documents typical of positivistic culture, attempted not only to establish a corpus of literary texts but also to articulate the poetics of travel literature.[1]

After a prolonged period of silence, research in this direction commenced again with particular intensity in the 1960s and continues unabated to the present day. During this time, numerous texts that dealt with the scientific discoveries or the expansionary phase of various European societies were edited or reprinted. This scholarship did not, however, consider travel literature either as a phenomenon having its own complex history or as one requiring critical distinctions to be made between the areas of study dealt with, the contents of their representation, and the forms adopted for their definition. But much has been done since these early studies. We are now in a better position to glean a picture of a genre (or a complex set of subgenres) as an object of theoretical speculation, which allows us to inquire about not only the relationships between language and research but also the development of the genre in connection with its authors, its public, its functions, and the means of its diffusion.

Italian travel literature of the nineteenth century seems to have been less understood than that of previous centuries. The reason for this discrepancy may be that the century was extremely diverse and complex. The material factors affecting the journeys undertaken, the means of communications employed, the organization of itineraries, and the social and cultural motives of the travelers themselves are by no means less complex and diverse than the historical conditions that gave rise to them.

As evidence of this complexity we need not look any further than the classic bio-bibliography of Amat di San Filippo. In it we find journeys of learned men, missionaries, antiquarians, artists, adventurers, scholars, naturalists, archaeologists, diplomats, explorers, soldiers, rich vagabonds, agriculturalists, writers, journalists, special correspondents, scientists, various government officials, to mention only the most important journeys

G. G. Cernecov. *I pittori russi al foro romano* (Russian painters at the Roman Forum). 1842. Oil on canvas, 85.5 x 110 cm. National Museum of Byelorussia, Minsk.

dealing with an expanding and constantly changing political reality that affected the transformation taking place in travel writing.

The first fifteen years of the century, wrote Amat di San Filippo, witnessed a reduction in the number of travelers. Political developments related to Napoleon's exploits curtailed significantly the frequency and types of journeys undertaken in Europe. The only exception to this decrease were those journeys initiated for military purposes, which resulted in essays and memoirs dealing with the historical fate of Europe.

Following the Napoleonic era, one notices an intensification in scientific exploration and commercial journeys. Egypt became an important point of reference.[2] Explorers specializing in geographical or other scientific disciplines made steady inroads into Africa and Asia. Interest in the New World increased, and many travelers journeyed not only to the Far East and Oceania but also to the Arctic. At the same time there was also a considerable increase in Italian scientific expeditions, organized in competition with those commissioned by foreign countries. A good number of these expeditions were undertaken under the aegis of the Navy and were organized for study purposes with military, diplomatic, and scientific objectives.

A work that significantly encouraged the undertaking of these expeditions was Pietro Amat di San Filippo's *Biografia dei viaggiatori italiani colla bibliografia delle loro opere.*[3] Amat's prefatory remarks in favor of these endeavors underlined a number of objectives and called upon the government of the new Italian State to devote special attention to these explorations. It was clear that, in this new climate, the cultural tradition of travel literature became intertwined with the commercial and scientific interests of Italy's new colonial policy, a development that pointed to a new function and potential of the genre.

It should be kept in mind that as far as traveling was concerned, the nineteenth century is of crucial importance. New forms of organized tourism and new means of communication developed rapidly, thereby facilitating the implementation of a colonial policy, which provided the stimulus for large-scale emigration.

For these reasons, nineteenth-century travel literature incorporates a great variety of models, forms, structures, and levels of language. An exhaustive history of this genre would require the collaboration of a wide range of specialists: historians, economic historians, historians of science and geography, literary critics, and journalists. My own competence is rather specialized and therefore insufficient to embrace the totality of the subject, but I shall give some paradigmatic examples representing the more common tendencies of the genre, in order to better appreciate the contribution many of the writers in question made to the formation of technical language.

Giuseppe Acerbi is an author who continues the tradition of the encyclopedic travel journal firmly rooted in the previous century. A controversial figure known to most people as the editor of the pro-Austrian periodical *Biblioteca Italiana*, Acerbi made his first journey abroad after 1798 when, following the arrival of the French in Italy, he went north to Lapland and the North Cape. He was later appointed Austrian consul in Cairo, where he studied natural sciences and archaeology.[4] He accompanied Champollion and Rosellini on their expeditions, and he presented Italian museums and libraries with findings of great value. The most important contribution of his many travels was the publication of numerous articles and an exhaustive volume, *Viaggi attraverso la Svezia, la Finlandia, e la Lapponia al Capo Nord negli anni 1798–99*, published in English in London in 1802 and immediately translated into German and French.[5]

This volume starts with a wide-ranging discussion about the reliability of reports and sources, the difficulty of distinguishing between reliable and unreliable information gleaned from local inhabitants, and the poor communications and facilities available to travelers journeying in the North. It follows the style of an eighteenth-century travel account, focusing on all the most important aspects of daily life. With meticulous attention given to the organization of his material and intelligently balancing his topics, the author delves into geography and landscape, economic resources, the political system, the climate, the personal and social customs. As the traveler makes his way northward into the most deserted and uninhabited areas, emphasis is given to the observations of meterological conditions, conditions of human and animal life, food, and landscape. Scientific observation is supported by data of various kinds. The first part of the journey is dominated by observations of the social stratification of the people and the enlightened monarchical system, particularly as it relates to the welfare of its subjects. The form of Acerbi's volume is that of a standard travel account, in which one finds progressively more critical analyses of unique as well as common features of the places he visited. His style although very even and linear has also the capacity to achieve intense lyricism, as is the case, for instance, during his description of the icy winter scenes in Stockholm or the frozen expanses of Lapland.

Acerbi's depiction of the countries he visited is essentially an analytical and objective representation. In Sweden he describes, for example, the country's geography and landscape, the progressive and contradictory features of its politics and culture, as well as the state of the arts. In Finland, instead, Acerbi laments the excessive urbanization of the country and the corresponding hedonistic values of its inhabitants:

> Hélas! je l'avoue: je n'ai pas toujours assez de philosophie pour être insensible moi-même aux plaisirs et aux biens que l'on croit trouver dans le tourbillon du monde; mais si nous réfléchissions aux suites déplorables de cette fièvre de désirs, née du rafinement [sic] des sociétés, et dont la brûlante chaleur porte de grands propriétaires à fuir des campagnes vers les cité populeuses pour échanger leur indépendance contre tant de frivolités . . . nous chercherions à nous dérober aux inquiétudes, aux anxiétés angoisses de ces grandes scènes de la vie, et . . . nous voudrions nous

soustraire à ces jouissances, toujours si vainement cherchées dans les tumultueuses réunions des peuples policés.

[Alas, I must confess: not always have I sufficient philosophy to be insensitive to the pleasures and benefits that the bustle of the world seems to offer. But were we to reflect upon the deplorable consequences of the fever of desires born of society's refinement, whose burning heat draws great landowners in a rush from the country to the populous cities to exchange their independence for so many frivolities . . . we should try to spare ourselves the worries, anxieties and anguish of these great scenes of life, and . . . we should wish to withdraw from the pleasures sought in vain by the tumultous gatherings of civilized peoples."][6]

As one can observe, Acerbi was a traveler whose interests were close to those of the encyclopedic travelers of the eighteenth century who had great curiosity for the problems afflicting society, including those concerning the weakening of the ancien régime. Acerbi saw, in the order and charm of nature, a contrast with the disorder and upheaval of the times. He was, in short, a man who looked back to the previous century with nostalgia and longing.

It may not be a coincidence, therefore, that Acerbi's subsequent writings, which dealt mainly with such topics as philology and archaeology, were undertaken with a renewed spirit of critical and scientific objectivity.[7]

By the end of the eighteenth century, the optimism of European encyclopedism had already been strongly challenged. The rigor of scientific research and specialization could now be seen as a possible defense against utopias and dreams, a form of protection against the dissolution of reason and against what seemed to be a difficult historical progress considered too rapid for orderly change.

Against this backdrop, the "philosophical" journey of the eighteenth century was replaced by accurate, well-informed, and scientific travel accounts. This process was the result of a willful negation of intellectual charisma and it took the form of the journey of an ignoramus. A remarkable work with this very title, *Il viaggio di un ignorante,* was published in Milan in 1857. The title went on to specify: *ossia ricetta per gli ipocondriaci composta dal dottore Giovanni Rajberti.* The author, a doctor who likened himself to a humorist, wrote satire and parody in the fashion of Lawrence Sterne, dealing with everyday life and bourgeois behavior. In his *Il viaggio di un ignorante,* edited and with a preface by Enrico Ghidetti, Rajberti suggested that travel be undertaken as a cure for the hypochondria of the bourgeoisie. He also advocated that journeys become the antidote for the excessive concern with fashion and superfluous erudition. By eliminating the myth of learning for the sake of learning, he thus privileges the "dear and sweet ignorance," the "virginity of the mind," the spontaneity of "common sense," and "the art of living with the world."[8]

These suggestions represented a complete reversal from the traditional approaches taken in preparation for journeys such as the Grand Tour. Rajberti wrote:

> Mi dicono di studiare la lingua per i viaggi. Oibò! Non si sa mai abbastanza la lingua propria, e si dovrà impacciarsi in quella dei forestieri? E poi dappertutto vi sono interpreti e servitori di piazza che parlano per noi: e per moltissime faccende bastano anche i gesti: i sordo-muti non esprimono qualunque idea senza la voce?
>
> [They tell me to study languages for traveling. Heavens! One never even knows one's own language well enough, so why should one meddle in the language of foreigners? And then everywhere there are interpreters and attendants in the square who speak for us: and for lots of things gestures are enough: don't the deaf and dumb manage to communicate all manner of ideas without using their voices?][9]

He goes on to further criticize the old prescriptions of travel manuals by highlighting, in the form of satire, the trivial and unessential information provided:

Ho da dire a qual grado di longitudine sia situata? Non me lo ricordo piú, cioè non ho mai cercato di saperlo. Ho da raccontare quanti giorni vi abbia passato sotto la pioggia, e quanti a vista di sole? Imiterei senza frutto quel buon vecchio di Lord Raglan che in Crimea ha perduto un esercito, ma lasciò tante indicazioni barometriche e termometriche su questa penisola deliziosa.

[Should I say what longitude it is? I don't remember anymore, that is, I never bothered to find out. Should I tell how many days it rained and how many days the sun shone? It would be pointless, like imitating that good old Lord Raglan who, in Crimea, lost an army but left many barometric and thermometric readings on that delightful peninsula.][10]

The journey of the respectable buffoon can now unfold, privately recounting personal vicissitudes. The apparently absurd and sparkling world of travel satire becomes an instrument for a critical penetration of the world visited. It also affords a viewpoint that is more complex and inspiring than that of the traditionally didactic travel story.

Il viaggio di un ignorante is a collection of essays satirizing the epistolary form of eighteenth-century journeys. It is a travel book that channels the informative elements of specific details into a satirical framework and places the author at the center of polemical stances. The memorialistic dimension—woven together with the travel theme and acting as the polemical voice—makes for a style that distinguishes itself from the many scientific, geographical, and environmental reports. While the scientific reports were increasingly in demand for scientific journals, travel reportages were published widely by newspapers and editors looking for contributions that successfully met the expectations of a more sophisticated reading public. Indeed, the publishing trade of the recently unified country not only tended to reflect the events taking place in middle-class Italian society but also encouraged interest in European and international affairs.

Important events like the Universal Exhibition of Vienna, in 1873, provided the necessary incentive for the domestic publishing industry to become involved in extranational developments. To this end, "the biggest editors, Treves and Sonzogno, had mobilized," as Matilde Dillon recalls, "writers, journalists, and technicians for correspondence destined for newspapers and illustrated albums, securing for themselves the names of greatest prestige."[11]

A case in point is Giovanni Faldella. Commissioned by the *Gazzetta Piemontese*, the author filed reports from Vienna with a confidently polemical spirit, as one can see in his volume *A Vienna*, purposely subtitled *Gita con il lapis*. Faldella undertook the writing of his reportage with a significantly new stylistic approach:

> Vocaboli del Trecento, del Cinquecento, della parlata toscana e piemontesismi; sulle rive del patetico piantato uno sghignazzo da buffone: tormentato il dizionario come un cadavere, con la disperazione di dargli vita mediante il canto, il pianoforte, la elettricità e il reobarbaro. . . . Così seguiterò finché avrò carta e fiato. Tale è il mio stile, come venne ridotto il mondo piccino . . . dai libri grossi.

> [Tuscan speech from the fourteenth and sixteenth centuries, as well as Piedmontese idiomatic expressions; on the verge of the pathetic, a buffoon lets out a guffaw; tormenting the dictionary like a corpse, desperately trying to give it life through singing, piano, electricity, and rhubarb. I shall go on like this as long as I have paper and breath. Such is my style, in the same way that the world was made small by large books.][12]

A "humoristic" writer, Faldella focuses on the comparison between his own provincial world and the Viennese and Parisian worlds he visited. By so doing he is instrumental not only in broadening the discussion of travel literature but also in creating a new awareness of Italy's relationship with the rest of Europe.

He achieves this through his own unique involvement over and above that provided by tourist guides of the past.

Faldella's range of travel articles, from those on Vienna in 1873 to those on Paris in 1887, is the expression of a unique "story-reportage," in which the verve of the writer is unleashed as he sketches personal portraits, captures atmospheres, and adds linguistic embellishments. Similar to Heinrich Heine's *Reisebilder*, Angelo Brofferio's *I Miei Tempi*, and Father Bresciani's *Lettere sul Tirolo tedesco*, the first of Faldella's works followed a journalistic model based on observation and aimed essentially at conveying information to his readers. However, in the second volume, entitled *A Parigi*, the author becomes more self-conscious about his style and less preoccupied with the informative elements of the work. The emphasis he places on the comic aspect of life gives color and tone to the movement of four characters as they journey from the village of Monticella in Piedmont to the French capital.

With *A Vienna* and *A Parigi*, the traditional reportage, argues Luigi Surdich, "undergoes revision and registers a widening of its own limits; it is thus connected to the territory of the story." More specifically, Faldella's approach reveals "a progressive lowering of the inventive 'verve' and of the verbal mixture which, from the uninterrupted use of more heterogeneous approaches in *A Vienna*, proceeds toward the impressionistic intermissions of *Viaggio a Roma*, and arrives at the more standard and formalized linguistic code of *A Parigi*."[13] Rich in digressions and insertions, the work reaches levels of signification that exceed those of the traditional reportage. Witness, for example, the humor of the final chapter, "Interruzione e fine," in which the author, by comparing the "provincials" with the Parisians, satirizes the new phenomenon of mass tourism:

> I nostri viaggiatori dovevano ancora visitare e studiare il Père Lachaise, il Salon, Versaglia, il Louvre e il Lussemburgo, i brodi di Duval, i teatri, il bosco di Boulogne, Goupil, la Morgue, Les Halles, quando giunse loro la notizia di una

tremenda inondazione che minacciava fino il campanile di Monticella.

[Our travelers still had to visit and study Père Lachaise, the Salon, Versailles, the Louvre and the Luxemburg, Duval's cuisine, the theaters, the Bois de Boulogne, Goupil, the Morgue, Les Halles, when news reached them of a terrible flood threatening even the bell tower at Monticella.][14]

It becomes apparent that this kind of prose has the limits of a self-contained game, and it is also apparent that, as Giorgio Ragazzini points out, "the anti-conformism of the language was not kept up by him out of any polemical intention, that he wanted to make of it the sign of a revolt both moral and political," sometimes with limits of a "goliardic extent."[15]

At the other end of the spectrum, one finds Edmondo De Amicis, whose reportage, despite its literary merit, has seldom met with critical approval. Contemporary critics, such as Carducci, saw in the work of "Capitano de Amicis" the last and "most ridiculous example of the imbecilic servility and impotent Italian stupidity of the Liberation period."[16] When comparing De Amicis's work to Faldella's, Carducci concludes that the latter's prose is far superior in both elegance and complexity. So superior are Faldella's literary merits, in fact, that Carducci proposes them as standards for imitation: "[many pages] are embellished, designed, sculpted, shaped, finished, as I wish imaginative Italian prose for children would always be."[17] Faldella's own evaluation of De Amicis is hardly flattering. He attacks his limited capacity by criticizing the "languid" tone of his prose:

> Quando i lettori paiono stracchi e sono ad un cece di sbadigliare le sue ideuzze, che fanno ritornello, al suo stile levigato tutto superficie, senza rialzi o rinfranchi di sintassi, tutto indicativi presenti, senza soggiuntivi o gerundii, egli dà una strizzatina alla spugna, ed ecco la damigella del villaggio, i sergenti furieri, i sindaci, gli studenti, le damine del buon-

tono, che lo leggono, piangono tutti, perché piange anch'egli seguendo il precetto muffoso di Orazio: *si vis me flere, flendum est ipsi tibi.*

[When the readers appear tired and are a tad away from yawning at his simple repeated ideas, his superficial polished style, unvaried and uninvigorated syntax, always in the present indicative, with no subjunctive or gerund, he manages to give the sponge another squeeze, to bring tears to the eyes of the village damsel, the quartermasters, the mayors, the students, the high-tone ladies, who read him, because he also is crying as he follows Horace's musty precept: *If you would have me weep, you must first weep yourself.*][18]

Faldella, however—contrary to Carducci's totally negative evaluation—insists on recognizing De Amicis's ability to reach a wide audience: "De Amicis è uno dei pochissimi scrittori italiani che sono entrati nel pubblico; e vi si è fatta una strada carreggiabile. Egli vi è penetrato per una porta scintillante di perle umide, per la porta del cuore" [De Amicis is one of very few Italian writers who have gained notoriety with the public; and he has opened a road that is easy to travel. He has got there through a doorway shining with pearl tears, through the doorway of the heart].[19]

In my own estimation, De Amicis remains an important travel writer who had a considerable influence on modern journalistic writing for his attempt to develop a unique style for the reportage. He dedicated much of his attention from 1871 onward toward this objective, both as a reader of travel and adventure books (he was an admirer of Verne and Stanley) and as an attentive traveler who wrote only from direct experience. The works of De Amicis must perforce be viewed as an integral part of a historical context that witnessed the emergence of many new journals, magazines, and special travel features, such as *Il Giro del Mondo. Giornale di Geografia; Viaggi e Costumi,* the Italian version of the famous *Tour de Monde,* published by Treves in

1863; and *Il Giornale Illustrato di Viaggi e delle Avventure di Terra e di Mare*, published by Sonzogno in 1878.

An analysis of De Amicis's works reveals a tendency to rely heavily on "colorismo," sentimentalism, and naïveté. All these features have been the target of many critics.[20] However, what must be underlined, is that De Amicis as a travel writer cannot be judged in monolithic fashion, but rather on the basis of his own individual development. The heavy dose of sentimentality, especially common in his early works, must be understood within the context of the author's didactic preoccupation. In contrast to the elitist practice of journalists of the period, De Amicis strove for the use of a simple language in order to better reach and instruct a wider public. From this point of view all his works, including the very early ones, reflect the author's bias that travel reports should be based upon the narration of facts and not on imaginative and fantastic experiences. This "new journalism" was meant to be used as a cultural instrument where the language employed was neither obscure nor unpleasant and was devoid of learned expressions. When reading works such as *Spagna* (1873), *Olanda* (1874), *Marocco* (1876), *Costantinopoli* (1878–79), *Ricordi di Parigi* (1879), *Sull'Oceano* (1889) and *La carrozza di tutti* (1899) we also become aware of a novel development in his narrative technique. Emotions are more controlled, sentimentality is less prevalent, and his capacity to draw attention to social problems is heightened.

Sull'Oceano shows De Amicis at his best. It is a report about the crossing of the Atlantic in 1884 by a group of immigrants bound for South America. So preoccupied was the author with these fundamental human problems that he continued to underscore their importance in other works. When invited to go to Buenos Aires by the *Nacional* he produced a remarkably sensitive reportage that highlighted the social tragedy of the immigrant experience.[21]

Another factor that must not be neglected in our evaluation of De Amicis is that the travel literature he produced also focused attention on the problems of modern urban life. *La carrozza di tutti* is a moving and impassioned reportage, which deals with the various social classes that make up the urban setting of Turin. It is an investigation of socioeconomic reality "in motion," as Giorgio Bertone wrote in his introduction to De Amicis's *Sull'Oceano*. According to Bertone, De Amicis gives a "moving portrait" of this city "at the time that electricity put the horse out to pasture, and in the year that inaugurated, together with the birth of an automobile factory, an era of different propulsion technologies, of new modes of transport and commuting, both urban and suburban."[22]

It is not by chance that the approach taken by De Amicis encouraged the young writer Renato Fucini to produce an exellent reportage from Naples in 1877. In the form of a diary, this reportage differed completely from anything the author was to produce later on. With a technique reminiscent of Dickens, Fucini paid close attention not only to the natural surroundings of the city, but also to the squalor of its working classes. Although conventional in its approach, his itinerary was undertaken "with a naked eye." Italo Calvino states that Fucini's work stands as "a document of how Italy after the Risorgimento became aware of the *internal frictions* of the country, which was just as disillusioned after its unification as it was hopeful prior to it."[23]

On the other hand, we also find editorials—reportage written by literary people inclined to produce learned, elegant, lively, and colorful articles—which lacked incisiveness when analyzing the world and society. Such articles, full of lyrical qualities and digressions, were a prelude to the features that would be typical of the cultural page of daily newspapers. Bearing this in mind, one can approach the travel reports written by Ferdinando Martini in "Fanfulla della Domenica." Martini was a follower of Carducci and his interests were mainly literary. He wrote as a journalist (which is evident in the famous article on Piedigrotta), but looked at the world of ordinary people with the condescending air of an aristocrat.[24] He was deeply moved by nature and ready to express his inner emotions in a lyrical mood.[25] In fact, the lyrical qualities of his writings stand as an example of the travel literature that was also produced in the second half of the nineteenth century and shows the relationship between journalism and literature. If, on the one hand, there is a journalistic prose that is heavily indebted to literary conventions, on the other hand, we witness the rise of travel reports—especially between the two world wars—that contributed to enrich and enliven so much "ornate prose," "Elzevirs," and the like.

Toward the end of the nineteenth and the beginning of the twentieth centuries travel literature had succeeded in generating discussion about the recently united Italy and highlighted the depth of the problems that still afflicted the country after 1870. It contributed significantly to the awareness of how unattainable were the expectations that the nation had placed upon political unity. The fragile economy of the newly created country, together with the fragmentary nature of its social and political institutions, were still obstacles that the young nation had not been able to overcome.

In this context, authors of travel literature became more relevant as they continued to draw attention to these problems. They were particularly suited to do so. Not only had they contributed significantly, as we have seen, to a new pragmatic view of social phenomena, but they had also, as a consequence, developed a language aptly suited to describe the problems in a more realistic way. Journeys, reportage, and travel manuals proliferated and sensitized an ever growing reading public, thus laying the basis for a greater appreciation and understanding of contemporary society.

Notes

Introduction: Spiritual Travelers in Western Literature

1. Genesis 16:12, in *The New English Bible*, ed. Samuel Sandmel (New York: Oxford University Press, 1976).
2. Proclus, *The Elements of Theology*, trans. and ed. E. R. Dodds (Oxford: Clarendon Press, 1933), props. 33, 146.
3. Plotinus, *The Six Enneads*, trans. Stephen MacKenna and B. S. Page (London: Faber and Faber, 1956), 1.6.8; see also 6.5.7, 6.5.10, 6.9.9.
4. Augustine, *The City of God*, trans. Marcus Dodds (New York: Hafner, 1948), 1.9.17.
5. *The Confessions of Saint Augustine*, trans. F. J. Sheed (London: Sheed and Ward, 1944), 12.16, 13.13.
6. John Bunyan, *The Pilgrim's Progress* (London: Zephyr Books, 1945), 157–58.
7. For a detailed treatment of the motif of the spiral journey in these and other writers of the early nineteenth century, see M. H. Abrams, *Natural Supernaturalism: Tradition and Revolution in Romantic Literature* (New York: Norton, 1971), chapters 4 and 5.
8. Thomas Carlyle, *Sartor Resartus*, ed. C. F. Harrold (New York: Odyssey Press, 1937), 147, 185, 188–89.
9. J. G. Fichte, *Grundriss des Eigenthümlichen der Wissenschaftslehre*, in *Sämtliche Werke*, ed. Fichte (Berlin, 1845), 1:332–33.
10. J. G. Fichte, *Die Grundzüge des gegenwärtigen Zeitalters*, in *Sämtliche Werke*, ed. Fichte, 7:12.
11. F. W. J. von Schelling, *System des transzendentalen Idealismus*, in *Sämtliche Werke* (Stuttgart, 1856–61), 2:341, 628. For other references to the *Iliad* and *Odyssey* as a two-part epic of spiritual departure and return, see ibid., 6:42, 57.
12. Friedrich Schiller, *On the Aesthetic Education of Man*, ed. and trans. Elizabeth M. Wilkinson and L. A. Willoughby (Oxford: Clarendon Press, 1967), 171; Schiller, "Über naive und sentimentalische Dichtung," in *Sämtliche Werke*, ed. Otto Güntter and George Witkowski (Leipzig, n.d.), 17:505–6.

13. William Wordsworth, *Home at Grasmere*, ed. Beth Darlington (Ithaca, N.Y.: Cornell University Press, 1977), ms. D, lines 45, 103–7.
  14. G. W. F. Hegel, *Phänomenologie des Geistes*, ed. Johannes Hoffmeister, 6th ed. (Hamburg: F. Meiner, 1952), 20, 26–27, 67, 563–64, 549; also, *The Logic of Hegel*, trans. William Wallace, 2d ed. (Oxford, 1892), 379.
  15. *The Logic of Hegel*, 379.
  16. William Wordsworth, *The Prelude*, ed. Ernest de Selincort (Oxford: Clarendon Press, 1926), 205.
  17. T. S. Eliot, *Collected Poems 1909–62* (London: Faber and Faber, 1963), 187–214.
  18. Ibid.

Chapter 1: Ugo Foscolo's Europe

Author's note: This paper reflects my research project on the sublime in Italian culture. For my previous publications on the same topic, see E. Mattioli, "Gli studi di Gustavo Costa sul Sublime in Italia," *Studi e Problemi di Critica Testuale* 36 (April 1988): 139–55.

  1. Ugo Foscolo, *Gli appunti per le "Lettere scritte dall'Inghilterra"* (Leghorn: Biblioteca Labronica, ms. 14, cc. 98v-143v, ed. L. Conti Bertini [Florence: La Nuova Italia, 1975]), xxv-lxxiii. On Foscolo's stay in England, see E. R. Vincent, *Ugo Foscolo: An Italian in Regency England* (Cambridge: Cambridge University Press, 1953). The validity of Vincent's book was duly stressed by an illustrious critic, who asserted that "one can do no better than refer to that biography" (Glauco Cambon, *Ugo Foscolo: Poet of Exile* [Princeton: Princeton University Press, 1980], 15.

  2. On Cesarotti's opinion of *Ortis*, and for Binni's interpretation, see G. Costa, "Melchiorre Cesarotti, Vico and the Sublime," *Italica* 58, no. 1 (Spring 1981): 10–11. On the sublime in *Ortis*, see A. Sole, "La sublimità malinconica di Jacopo Ortis," *Rassegna della Letteratura Italiana* n.s. 88, nos. 1–2 (January-August 1984): 52–79. Unfortunately, Sole fails to identify the specific character of Foscolo's sublime within the context of contemporary culture. Foscolo himself acknowledged his debt to *Werther* in a letter he addressed to Goethe (16 January 1802): see *Ultime lettere di Jacopo Ortis*, ed. Giovanni Gambarin, vol. 4, *Edizione Nazionale delle Opere di Ugo Foscolo* (Florence: Le Monnier, 1955), 542. In 1803, the *Giornale dell'Italiana Letteratura* compared *Ortis* to *Werther*: see G. Avanzi and G. Sichel, *Bibliografia italiana su*

Goethe (1779–1965) (Florence: Olschki, 1972), no. 15, 3; E. Guidorizzi, *L'Italia, Goethe e la natura: la critica letteraria italiana* (Naples: ESI, 1980), 14–15. On the *Werther-Ortis* relation, see Giuliano Manacorda, *Materialismo e masochismo: Il "Werther," Foscolo e Leopardi* (Florence: La Nuova Italia, 1973), 27–36; and G. Nicoletti, *Il "metodo" dell'"Ortis" e altri studi foscoliani* (Florence: La Nuova Italia, 1978), 41–70. For Sterne's influence on Foscolo, see L. Berti, *Foscolo traduttore di Sterne* (Florence: Edizioni di Rivoluzione, 1942); P. Fasano, "L'amicizia con Sterne e la traduzione didimea del *Sentimental Journey*," in *Stratigrafie foscoliane* (Rome: Bulzoni, 1974), 83–189; Claudio Varese, *Foscolo: sternismo, tempo e persona* (Ravenna: Longo, 1982).

3. See Costa, "Foscolo e la poetica del sublime," *Forum Italicum* 12, no. 14 (Winter 1978): 483.

4. Foscolo, *Poesie e carmi: Poesie—Dei sepolcri—Poesie postume—Le Grazie*, ed. F. Pagliai, G. Folena, and M. Scotti, vol. 1: *Edizione Nazionale delle Opere di Ugo Foscolo* (Florence: Le Monnier, 1987), 1098.

5. Longinus, *On the Sublime*, ed. and trans. W. R. Roberts, 2d ed. (Cambridge: Cambridge University Press, 1935), 82–83.

6. Foscolo, *Lezioni, articoli di critica e di polemica (1809–1811)*, in *Edizione Nazionale delle Opere di Ugo Foscolo*, ed. E. Santini (Florence: Le Monnier, 1933), 7:226. Part of the same passage was quoted by Foscolo in his *Ragguaglio d'un'adunanza dell'Accademia de' Pitagorici* (1810): see ibid., 242.

7. Foscolo, *Prose varie d'arte*, ed. Mario Fubini, vol. 5: *Edizione Nazionale delle Opere di Ugo Foscolo* (Florence: Le Monnier, 1951), 359.

8. Lord Byron, *Don Juan*, ed. T. G. Steffan, E. Steffan, and W. W. Pratt (New Haven and London: Yale University Press, 1982), 41.

9. *Horn of Oberon: Jean Paul Richter's School for Aesthetics*, trans. M. R. Hale (Detroit: Wayne State University Press, 1973), 88. See Costa, "Il comico e il sublime nella cultura del primo Settecento," *Intersezioni* 1 (1981): 555–73. Richter's Romantic humor practically coincides with Romantic irony, which has been the object of numerous studies. See, for instance, A. K. Mellor, *English Romantic Irony* (Cambridge, Mass.: Harvard University Press, 1980); L. R. Furst, *Fictions of Romantic Irony* (Cambridge, Mass.: Harvard University Press, 1984); and D. J. Enright, *The Alluring Problem: An Essay on Irony* (Oxford and New York: Oxford University Press, 1986). I share Almansi's distaste for the "tragicisti, i quali presumono di teorizzare il territorio dell'arte solo dall'al-

topiano del sublime e non dalla bassura di ciò che suscita riso e diletto" [tragedians who presume they can theorize about the realm of the arts only from the heights of the sublime, not from the depths wherein lies the inspiration for laughter and delight]; G. Almansi, *La ragion comica* (Milan: Feltrinelli, 1986), 10. However, I also believe that no serious student of the comic should ignore the implications of the sublime.

10. *Plutarch's Moralia in Fifteen Volumes*, vol. 7, ed. and trans. P. H. De Lacy and B. Einarson (London: Heinemann; Cambridge, Mass.: Harvard University Press, 1959), 520–21.

11. Ibid., 520–23. See *Euripides*, vol. 3, ed. and trans. A. S. Way (London: Heinemann; Cambridge, Mass.: Harvard University Press, 1950), 374–75.

12. Mario Scotti, "I primi cinque anni del Foscolo inglese, attraverso l'epistolario," in *Foscolo fra erudizione e poesia* (Rome: Bonacci, 1973), 127. See also Gustavo Costa, "Due inediti foscoliani," *Modern Language Notes* 86, no. 1 (January 1971): 89–95.

13. Foscolo, *Prose varie*, 261. Edoardo Sanguineti remarked that Foscolo "confuse, citando a memoria, le parti di Polinice e di Giocasta" [quoting from memory, confused the parts of Polynices and Jocasta] in Foscolo, *Lettere scritte dall'Inghilterra. Gazzettino del Bel Mondo*, ed. E. Sanguineti (Milan: Mursia, 1978), no. 2, 28.

14. Foscolo, *Prose varie*, 263.

15. Ibid.

16. Ibid., 240. E. Mandruzzato observed that the *Lettere* is characterized by "un estro" [a flair] which Foscolo "credeva arguto perché lieto" [considered witty because light-hearted], although it lacks "lievità" [light-heartedness] and "indifferenza di fondo del vero umorismo" [deep seated indifference to true humor]. See Mandruzzato, *Foscolo* (Milan: Rizzoli, 1978), 392. What Mandruzzato means by "vero umorismo" is not clear to me. Certainly, he does not refer to Romantic humor.

17. Foscolo, *Prose varie*, 176.

18. Lawrence Sterne, *The Life and Opinions of Tristram Shandy, Gentleman*, ed. G. Petrie (Harmondsworth: Penguin, 1979), 33.

19. Foscolo, *Prose varie*, 39.

20. Sterne, *Tristram Shandy*, 79. On Sterne's attitude toward Longinus, see J. L. Lamb, "The Comic Sublime and Sterne's Fiction," *Journal of English Literary History* 48, no. 1 (Spring 1981): 110–43.

21. In his *Essay on Criticism*, 675–80, Pope pays homage to "bold Longinus" who, being a critic and a poet at the same time, was the

incarnation of the sublime: "and is himself that Great Sublime he draws" (*The Poems of Alexander Pope*, ed. J. Butt [New Haven: Yale University Press, 1963]), 165.

˚22. F. Gritti, *Memorie del Signor Tommasino*, ed. R. Damiani (Milan: Curcio, 1979), 119. See G. Ficara, "Rousseau e cioccolata nel caffé veneziano," *Tuttolibri* 5, no. 15 (21 April 1979): 11.

23. Romantic humor in Alfieri's *Vita*, as treated in my paper "Achilles and Thersites in the Maelstrom of the French Revolution: The Sublime and the Ludicrous in Alfieri's *Vita*" (originally read at the seventeenth annual meeting of the Western Society for Eighteenth-century Studies, University of California, Berkeley, 18–19 February 1989, unpublished).

24. Foscolo, *Prose varie*, 334.

25. Alfieri, *Vita scritta da esso*, ed. L. P. Fassò (Asti: Casa d'Alfieri, 1951), 1:110–15.

26. Foscolo, *Prose varie*, 334. On Foscolo's fall from his horse, see Foscolo, *Epistolario*, ed. Mario Scotti, *Edizione Nazionale delle Opere di Ugo Foscolo* (Florence: Le Monnier, 1970), 208, no. 1.

27. Ibid., 223.

28. Alfieri, *Vita*, 1:213.

29. Foscolo, *Prose varie*, 174.

30. Foscolo, *Prose politiche e letterarie dal 1811 al 1816: Frammenti sul Machiavelli, Ipercalisse, Storia del sonetto, Discorsi sulla servitù dell'Italia, Scritti vari*, ed. L. P. Fassò, vol. 8: *Edizione Nazionale delle Opere di Ugo Foscolo* (Florence: Le Monnier, 1933), 105.

31. Foscolo, *Prose varie*, 178.

32. Ibid., 298.

33. Ibid.

34. Ibid.

35. Ibid.; see Foscolo, *Prose politiche*, 99–100.

36. Foscolo, *Prose politiche*, 100.

37. Foscolo, *Epistolario*, 7:289.

38. Ibid.

39. Foscolo, *Gli appunti*, 26.

40. Foscolo, *Prose varie*, 412.

41. Ibid., 244–45.

42. Ibid., 288.

43. This is the *incipit* of the final version of the *Ortis*, which Foscolo published in Zurich in 1816 (with the false imprint of London 1814). This edition reproduces, with a minor modification, the beginning of

the novel as it was printed in Milan in 1802. The 1798 edition published in Bologna had quite a different opening: "Sia dunque cosí! io vivrò lontano da quanto m'avea di piú caro" [So be it! I shall live far away from the things I held dearest]. See Foscolo, *Ultime lettere*, 5, 137, 295.
44. Foscolo, *Prose varie*, 285–86.
45. B. Croce and F. Nicolini, *Bibliografia vichiana* (Naples: Ricciardi, 1947–48), 1:425–27; G. Cambon, "Vico e Foscolo," *Forum Italicum* 12, no. 4 (Winter 1978): 498–511.
46. Foscolo, *Prose varie*, 383.
47. Ibid., 384.
48. Ibid., 385.
49. Ibid., 180.
50. Ibid., 385.
51. Ibid.
52. Longinus, *On the Sublime*, 14, 82.
53. Foscolo, *Prose varie*, 375.
54. Ibid., 281. Foscolo alludes to his fragments on the veil: see *Poesie e carmi*, 823–58.

Chapter 2: The Italian Journey

1. Leon Edel, *The Life of Henry James*, vol. 2: *The Conquest of London: 1870–81* (New York: Avon, 1978), 116, 126.
2. "De Gustibus—," "By the Fireside"; for the text of Browning's poems, see John Pettigrew's edition (New Haven and London: Yale University Press, 1981). For the text of *Daniel Deronda*, see Barbara Hardy's edition (Harmondsworth and New York: Penguin, 1967). For the text of *The Portrait of a Lady*, see Robert D. Bamberg's edition (New York: Norton, 1975). Quotations from James not otherwise identified are from his preface to the novel.
3. W. D. Shaw, "Browning's Duke as Theatrical Producer," *Victorian Newsletter* 29 (1966): 18–22.
4. F. R. Leavis, *The Great Tradition* (Garden City, N.Y.: Doubleday, 1954), 109.
5. Northrop Frye, *Anatomy of Criticism: Four Essays* (Princeton: Princeton University Press, 1957), 215.
6. See volume 1 of John Pettigrew's Yale edition of Browning's poems, 1078.
7. John Hollander, *The Figure of Echo: A Mode of Allusion in Milton and After* (Berkeley and Los Angeles: University of California Press,

1981); Christopher Ricks, "Tennyson Inheriting the Earth," in *Studies in Tennyson*, ed. Hallam Tennyson (London: Macmillan, 1981).

8. James Merrill, *Recitative: Prose by James Merrill* (San Francisco: North Point Press, 1986), 27.

9. M. H. Abrams, *Natural Supernaturalism: Tradition and Revolution in Romantic Literature* (New York: Norton, 1971), 246.

Chapter 3: Giacomo Leopardi

1. Giacomo Leopardi, *Zibaldone*, 1, 411, ed. Francesco Flora (Milan: Mondadori, 1957).

2. Monaldo Leopardi, in a letter to Antonio Ranieri. Printed by Francesco Flora in his edition of Giacomo Leopardi, *Canti, con una scelta di prosa* (Milan: Mondadori, 1959).

3. Leopardi, *Zibaldone*, 1:161–62.

4. Ibid., 100.

5. Leopardi, *Zibaldone*, 2:976.

6. Leopardi, "A Silvia," in Leopardi, *Canti*. All poems cited are from this work.

7. In a letter to Benjamin Bailey, 22 November 1817. See John Keats, *Complete Poems and Selected Letters*, ed. Clarence DeWitt Thorpe (New York: Doubleday, Doran, 1935), 523–26.

8. William Wordsworth, "Ode on the Intimations of Immortality," in Wordsworth, *Complete Poetical Works* (New York: Crowell, 1962), 403–6.

9. Ibid.

10. Leopardi, "Aspasia."

11. Samuel Taylor Coleridge, "Dejection: An Ode," in *The Poetical Works of Samuel Taylor Coleridge*, ed. James Dykes Campbell (London: Macmillan, 1893), 159–62.

12. Wordsworth, preface to *Lyrical Ballads*, in *Selected Prose*, ed. with intro. and notes by John O. Hayden (Harmondsworth: Penguin, 1988), 278–307.

13. Leopardi, *Zibaldone*, 1:488.

14. Leopardi, "La ginestra."

15. Hardy, "He Resolves to Say No More." See Thomas Hardy, *Winter Words in Various Moods and Metres* (London: Macmillan, 1928), 202.

16. Edwin Muir, *Essays on Literature and Society* (Cambridge, Mass.: Harvard University Press, 1967).

17. Leopardi, "Dialogo di Tristano e di un amico," in Leopardi, *Ope-*

rette Morali. Essays and Dialogues, ed. Giovanni Cecchetti (Berkeley and Los Angeles: University of California Press, 1982), 484–507.

18. Dante, *Inferno*, 15.87.
19. Leopardi, "La ginestra."
20. Wordsworth, preface to *The Excursion*, 457–64.
21. Leopardi, "Canto notturno"; Wordsworth, *The Prelude*, 3.291, 5.301.
22. Leopardi, "Ad Angelo Mai."
23. Leopardi, "Bruto minore."
24. Leopardi, "Alla luna."
25. Leopardi, "Canto notturno."
26. Leopardi, "La quiete dopo la tempesta."
27. Leopardi, "Sopra il ritratto di una bella donna."
28. Leopardi, "Il tramonto della luna."
29. Leopardi, "La ginestra."
30. Wordsworth, "Lines Composed a Few Miles above Tintern Abbey," in Wordsworth, 115–18.
31. Leopardi, *Zibaldone*, 1:1169.
32. Leopardi, "Al conte Carlo Pepoli."
33. Robert Browning, *Pippa Passes*, part 1 (London: Duckworth, 1898).
34. Leopardi, "A Silvia."
35. Leopardi, "La ginestra."
36. Leopardi, "Canto notturno."
37. Leopardi, "La ginestra."
38. Ibid.
39. Leopardi, *Zibaldone*, 1:68.
40. Leopardi, "A se stesso."
41. Leopardi, "La ginestra."
42. Leopardi, "Le ricordanze."
43. Edward Fitzgerald, *Rubáiyát of Omar Khayyám and Six Plays of Calderon* (London: J. M. Dent, 1948).

Chapter 4: Of Swallows and Farewells

1. Cf. J. Campbell, *The Hero with a Thousand Faces* (Princeton: Princeton University Press, 1949); and V. Propp, *Morphology of the Folktale* (Austin: University of Texas Press, 1968).
2. If science has succeeded to some extent in deallegorizing move-

ment, not so literature, which traditionally has been perceived as repository and manifestation of values inherent in a certain culture. For the scientific aspect, cf. G. Holton, "Science and the Deallegorization of Motion," in *The Nature and Art of Motion*, ed. G. Kepes (New York: Braziller, 1965), 25–31; and also G. Dorfles, "The Role of Motion in Our Visual Habits and Artistic Creation," ibid., 41–50.

3. Thomas Cook, who had been organizing railway excursions in the Midlands for ten years, in 1855 arranged a special trip to Paris, and soon after the Cook Tours began bringing Englishmen to Europe (especially France and Italy). The introduction in 1873 of the sleeping car (an American invention) facilitated leisure travel even further.

4. Cf. G. Bàrberi Squarotti, "Partenza o fuga: da Renzo e Lucia ad Anguilla," *Lettere italiane* (1976): 160–77; S. B. Chandler, "The Motif of the Journey in the Eighteenth-century Novel in Scott and in Manzoni," *Rivista di Studi Italiani* (December 1985): 1–10.

5. "Conclusero che i guai vengono bensí spesso, perché ci si è dato cagione; ma che la condotta piú cauta e piú innocente non basta a tenerli lontani; e che quando vengono, o per colpa o senza colpa, la fiducia in Dio li raddolcisce, e li rende utili per una vita migliore" [They concluded that troubles indeed come often, because we bring them upon ourselves, but even the most cautious and most innocent conduct is not enough to keep them away; and when troubles do come, whether we are at fault or not, faith in God can assuage them, and turn them to good use for a better life]; *I promessi sposi,* ed. Luigi Russo (Florence: La Nuova Italia, 1966), 725.

6. "Ho imparato . . . a non mettermi ne' tumulti: ho imparato a non predicare in piazza: ho imparato a guardare con chi parlo: ho imparato a non alzar troppo il gomito: ho imparato a non tenere in mano il martello della porta, quando c'è lì d'intorno gente che ha la testa calda: ho imparato a non attaccarmi un campanello al piede, prima d'aver pensato quel che ne possa nascere" [I have learned . . . not to get involved in public demonstrations: I have learned not to preach in the square: I have learned to be careful with whom I talk: I have learned not to drink too much: I have learned not to hold on to the door knocker, when there are hot headed people around: I have learned not to tie a bell to my foot without first thinking what could possibly come of it]; *I promessi sposi,* 725.

7. From the sonnet by Foscolo, "In morte del fratello Giovanni," 1–2:2

8. Ovid, *Tristia*, 5.7.61–68.
9. Cf. G. Cambon, *Ugo Foscolo: Poet of Exile* (Princeton: Princeton University Press, 1980).
10. Leopardi, "Dialogo di Cristoforo Colombo e di Pietro Gutierrez" in Giacomo Leopardi, *Operette morali*, ed. Mario Fubini (Turin: Loescher, 1983), 209–16.
11. Leopardi, "Dialogo di un fisico e di un metafisico," ibid., 125–33.
12. Leopardi, "Dialogo della Terra e della Luna," ibid., 106–13.
13. Leopardi, "Cantico del gallo silvestre," ibid., 226–31.
14. Cf. the anthology *Memorialisti dell'Ottocento*, 3 vols. (Milan: Ricciardi, n.d.).
15. Cf. the anthology *I poeti minori dell'Ottocento*, 2 vols. (Milan: Ricciardi, n.d.).
16. It would be difficult to find in the Italian literature of the *Ottocento* a title similar to Leonard Sidney Woolf's title for his autobiography: *The Journey, Not the Arrival, Matters* (London: Hogarth, 1969).
17. *Addio al Parnaso* (Milan: Bompiani, 1971), 8.
18. On this topic, see A. Bianchini, *Il romanzo d'appendice* (Turin: ERI, 1969); M. Romano, *Mitologia romantica e letteratura popolare: struttura e sociologia del romanzo d'appendice* (Ravenna: Longo, 1977); A. A. Veronese, *Dame, droga e galline. Romanzo popolare e romanzo di consumo tra '800 e '900* (Padua: CLEUP, 1977); G. Zaccaria, *Il romanzo d'appendice: aspetti della narrativa popolare nei secoli XIX e XX* (Turin: Paravia, 1977).
19. I take that term from Wolfgang Iser, to indicate an utterance "which actually creates its object," as opposed to "constative utterance," which "describes an object that exists with equal determinacy ouside it." Cf. "Indeterminacy and the Reader's Response in Prose Fiction" in *Aspects of Narrative*, ed. J. Hillis Miller (New York: Columbia University Press, 1971), 7; and Iser, *The Implied Reader* (Baltimore: Johns Hopkins University Press, 1974).
20. "Fumatori di carta," in *Poesie edite e inedite* (Turin: Einaudi, 1962), 31.
21. See G. Celati, *Finzioni occidentali: fabulazione comicità e scrittura* (Turin: Einaudi, 1975), esp. 28–31.
22. G. Rodari, "I viaggi di Pulcinella," *Filastrocche in cielo e in terra* (Turin: Einaudi, 1960), 53.
23. But even after being demoralized, cultural habits have a tendency to linger, perhaps even as mere life-style preferences. In a recent survey

("Estate pigra per gli italiani") [Lazy summer for the Italians] published in *Donnapiù*, Lisa Corva wrote that "l'italiano, più che un viaggiatore, è un *vacanziere*" [the Italian more than a traveler, is a vacationer]. To explain that statement, Ettore Mazzotti, the editor of *Weekend*, said, "Da noi la cultura del viaggio non esiste: gli italiani si spostano soltanto per cercare il mare e il sole, visti possibilmente dalla finestra di un buon albergo. Non hanno il piacere della scoperta, o dell'avventura: quel che a loro interessa è la comodità" [In Italy, the tradition of the journey does not exist: Italians travel only to find the sea or the sun, possibly viewed through the window of a good hotel. They find no pleasure in discovery, or in adventure: what they are interested in is comforts]; *Donnapiù* (July-August 1987): 36–37.

Chapter 5: Italie-Italies

1. Y. Hersant, *Italies, anthologie des voyageurs français au XVIIIe et XIXe siècles* (Paris: Laffont, 1988)—a work consisting of more than one thousand pages—has served as a basic reference for this essay. For the bibliography concerning French journeys to Italy, see J. Blane, *Bibliographie italo-française universelle*, 2 vols. (Milan, 1866); G. Lodovici, "Bibliografia dei viaggiatori stranieri in Italia nel secolo XIX," *Annales Institutorum Urbis Romae* 7 (1934–35): 241–60; G. Menichelli, *Viaggiatori francesi reali e immaginari nell'Italia dell'Ottocento. Primo saggio bibliografico* (Rome: Edizioni di Storia e Letteratura, 1962); J. D. Candeaux, "La bibliographie des voyages en Italie: état présent et perspectives d'avenir," *Bollettino del C.I.R.V.I.* (1980): 3–12; C. de Seta, "L'Italia nello specchio del *Grand Tour*," in *Storia d'Italia. Annali* 5 (Turin: Einaudi, 1982), 127–264; E. Chevalier and R. Chevalier, *Iter italicum* (Geneva: Slatkine, 1989); F. Claudon, *Le voyage romantique* (Paris: Lebaud, 1986).

2. Some of these authors are Alphonse Dupré, occasional poet and author of *Relation d'un voyage en Italie, suivie d'observations sur les Anciens et les Modernes* (Paris: Boucher, 1824); Arsène Houssaye (1815–96) novelist, playwright, poet, art and literary critic, journalist, and author of *Voyage à Venise* (Paris: Sartorius, 1850); Jules Janin (1804–74), journalist, author of *Voyages en Italie* (Paris: Bourdin, 1839); Paul Edme de Musset (1804–80), brother of Alfred, novelist, historian, author of *En voiturin, courses en Italie et en Sicile*, published posthumously in 1885. Anonymous author of *Voyage à Rome*; Hersant, *Italies*.

3. Those who undertake journeys follow closely upon the footsteps

of artists, scholars, musicians (especially after the founding of the Académie de France in Rome in 1666), clergymen, diplomats, and writers.

4. The journey as entertainment is clearly defined by Guy de Maupassant: "J'ai quitté Paris et même la France, parce-que la tour Eiffel finisait par m'ennuyer trop" [I left Paris and France altogether, because I ended up too bored with the Eiffel tower]; *La vie errante*, 1889, 227.

5. Discovered in 1770, Michel Montaigne's travel journal was edited and reprinted many times when the Grand Tour was at its most fashionable.

6. Maxmilien Misson, *Nouveau voyage d'Italie* (The Hague, 1691), a manual that Stendhal defines as "witty" and "excellent." Joseph-Jérôme de Lalonde, *Voyage d'un Français en Italie fait dans les années 1765 et 1766* (Venice and Paris: Desaint, 1769), a work that despite its thoroughness, or perhaps because of it, Stendhal defines as "plat" [flat] and Chateaubriand describes as "décharné" [meager]. R. de Saint-Non, *Voyage pittoresque ou Description du royaume de Naples et de Sicile* (Paris, 1781–86).

7. The presence of the many branch lines under construction in the Po Valley was a sign of the industrial growth underway.

8. For Théophile Gautier, these journeys served to compare the various Mediterranean countries: "Certes, la manie des comparaisons est un travers d'esprit, et il est injuste de demander à un endroit d'en être un autre; mais nous ne pouvons nous empêcher . . . de penser à ces belles sierras espagnoles, dont personne ne parle et dont la beauté ignorée est bien au-dessus des sites italiens, trop vantés peut-être" [Certainly the mania for making comparisons is a quirk of the spirit, and it is unjust to ask of a place to be another; but I cannot stop myself from thinking of those beautiful Spanish sierras, which no one talks about, whose overlooked beauty far surpasses the beauty of the Italian countryside, that is perhaps praised too much]; *Voyage en Italie*, 1850, 413.

9. "Un tronçon de chemin de fer nous mena jusqu'à Treviglio; la diligence continuant le wagon nous fit traverser de nuit Brescia; où l'on s'arrêta une heure" [We reached Treviglio on a branch line of the railway. We continued on a stage coach that took us through Brescia at night where we stopped for an hour]; ibid., 174, where one sees how the modern means of travel limit the freedom of the traveler.

10. Ibid., 180. The view of the canal from the hotel room is the same as the one that Chateaubriand had seen.

11. "Repassant dans notre tête la Venise de Canaletto, de Bonington,

de Joyant et de Wyld" [Reminiscing about the Venice of Canaletto, Bonington, Joyant, and Wyld]; ibid., 181.

12. "Notre premier soin fut de louer une gondole. On a beaucoup abusé de la gondole dans les opéras comiques, les romances et les nouvelles. Ce n'est pas une raison pour qu'elle soit mieux connue. Nous en ferons ici une description détaillée. La gondole est une production naturelle de Venise, un être animé ayant sa vie spéciale et locale, une espèce de poisson qui ne peut subsister que dans l'eau d'un canal. La lagune et la gondole sont inséparables et se complètent l'une par l'autre. Sans gondole, Venise n'est pas possible. La vie est un madrépore dont la gondole est le mollusque" [My first concern was to hire a gondola. The gondola has been terribly abused in comic operas, novel, and romances. This is no reason why it ought to be better known. I shall here make a detailed description of it. The gondola is naturally associated with Venice, an animate being having its own peculiar local existence, a type of fish that can survive only in the waters of a canal. The lagoon and the gondola are inseparable, they complement each other. Without the gondola, Venice is inconceivable. The city is a madrepore of which the gondola is the mollusk]; ibid., 181.

13. "Un cercle laissé libre au centre du rassemblement nous permet de voir un pauvre diable fort délabré, coiffé d'un chapeau élégiaque, vêtu d'un habit piteux et d'un pantalon effrangé; il a près de lui une vieille, affreuse compagnonne, parce que mêlée de sorcière, en aussi piètre équipage que le bonhomme" [A round opening in the middle of the gathering allows me to see a poor devil, very shabby, with a sad-looking hat, wearing a pitiful jacket and fraying pants; he has beside him an old and frightful woman campanion, a touch of the sorceress, as pitifully dressed as the gentleman]; ibid., 196. This generic description is typical of the topos of the Italian beggar.

14. "La femme de Ser Zuane, qui paraît jouir au logis d'une autorité despotique, est une grosse commère réjouie, haute en couleurs, bastionnée d'appas formidables" [The wife of Mr. Zuane, who seems to enjoy at the lodging a despotic authority, is a large and merry busybody, with rosy cheeks, and endowed with great feminine charm]; ibid., 198. A different type of Italian woman based on the image of the *mamma*.

15. "Cette grâce familière du bas peuple de Venise, dont la courtoise n'a rien de servile" [That simple grace of the common people of Venice, whose courtesy has nothing servile about it]; ibid., 199. A topos of the natural virtues of the Italian people.

Republic, see "Venise est là, assise sur le rivage de la mer, comme une belle femme qui va s'éteindre avec le jour: le vent du soir soulève ses cheveux embaumés; elle meurt, saluée par toutes les grâces et tous les sourires de la nature" [Venice is there, sitting on the seashore, like a beautiful woman who will perish with the day: the evening wind lifts her embalmed hair; she dies, proclaimed by all the graces and the smiles of nature]; ibid., 342.

29. Houssaye, *Voyage à Venice*, 355, 357. Georges Sand, *Lettres d'un voyage*, 353, 351. "Je défie qui que soit de m'empêcher de dormir agréablement quand je vois Venise, si appauvrie, si opprimée et si misérable" [I defy whoever it may be to prevent me from sleeping peacefully when I see Venice, so impoverished, so oppressed, and so wretched]; ibid., 351.

30. "L'ilôt de *San Giorgio* est en face avec son église et son campanile qui semble flotter sur la lagune; à droite s'élèvent la *Dogana di mar* et la *Salute*" [The isle of *San Giorgio* is opposite its church and its bell tower, which seems to float on the lagoon; on the right rise the *Dogana di mar* and the *Salute*]; ibid., 360. The view from Sand's window was similar to that of Chateaubriand.

31. Hippolyte Taine, *Voyage en Italie*, 370, 372. "Pareille à la fantaisie d'un magicien, au décor aérien d'un palais imaginaire, on aperçoit la place, avec ses colonnes, son campanile, entre deux cordons de lumière. Puis la barque s'engage dans des ruelles suspectes, où, de loin en loin, un falot projette sur l'eau son aigrette flageolante" [Similar to the imagination of a magician, to the airy decor of an imaginary palace, the place can be seen, with its columns, its bell tower, between two ribbons of light. Then the boat turns down suspicious alleyways, where at long intervals, a lantern projects its flickering ray upon the water]; ibid., 367.

32. Gautier, *Italia*, 167; Gautier, *Voyage en Italie*, 85.

33. Edgar Quinet, *Allemagne et Italie, philosophie et poésie*, 1016; Gautier, *Italia*, 338, 1016.

34. Gautier, *Italia*, 415.

35. Gautier, *Voyage en Italie*, 103. "Le Tibre sépare les deux gloires: assises dans la même poussière, Rome païenne s'enforce de plus en plus dans ses tombeaux, et Rome chrétienne redescend peu à peu dans les catacombes d'où elle est sortie" [The Tiber separates the two glories: sitting in the same dust, pagan Rome sinks more and more into its tombs and Christian Rome redescends little by little into the catacombs whence it came]; ibid., 93.

36. "Mais aussitôt que le soleil disparut à l'horizon, la cloche du dôme de Saint-Pierre retentit sous les portiques du Colisée. Cette correspondance établie par des sons religieux entre les deux plus grands monuments de Rome païenne et de Rome chrétienne me causa une vive émotion: je songeai que l'édifice moderne tomberait comme l'édifice antique; je songeai que les monuments se succèdent comme les hommes qui les ont élevés" [But as soon as the sun disappeared over the horizon, the bell from the dome of Saint Peter's resounded beneath the porticos of the Colosseum. This correspondence established by holy sounds between the two greatest monuments of pagan and Christian Rome caused me an acute sensation: I dreamed that the modern edifice would crumble as the ancient edifice had done; I dreamed that the monuments would follow each other as the man who had raised them]; ibid., 107.

37. Ibid., 97ff.

38. "Il y avait au milieu de tout cela, un enfant, vêtu non pas d'une chemise, mais d'une espèce de toile d'araignée à mille trous, qui n'avait pas d'écuelle et qui pleurait de faim" [There was in the middle of all this a child, wearing not a shirt but a sort of spider's web of a thousand holes, who did not have a bowl and who was crying from hunger]; A. Dumas, *Le Capitaine Arena*, 736, 865–66. Gautier, too, unknowingly revealed the reason for his compatriot's fascination for the figure of the brigand: "On nous dit qu'on allait fusiller sept brigands. . . . Si le temps ne nous eût manqué, nous aurions été voir cette exécution . . . car en voyage la curiosité va quelquefois jusqu'à la barbarie, et les yeux qui cherchent le nouveau ne se détournent pas d'un supplice si le bourreau est pittoresque et si le patient est d'une bonne couleur locale" [I was told that they were going to put seven brigands before the firing squad . . . If I had not been so short of time, I would have gone to see this execution . . . because, when traveling, curiosity sometimes comes very close to barbarity, and one's eyes, looking for new experiences, do not turn away from torture if the executioner is picturesque and if the sufferer is part of good local color"]; Gautier, *Voyage en Italie*, 176.

39. "Quant au *jettatore*, son essence est purement italienne. . . . Le *jettatore* a une de ces figures hétéroclites comme le climat de l'Italie en produit beaucoup; maigre, maladif et ridé, avec un long bec d'oiseau surmonté d'une paire de lunettes, la main osseuse, la bouche sardonique, il flotte dans ses larges vêtements" [As for the *jettatore*, his essence is purely Italian. . . . The *jettatore* is one of those anomalous figures that are found so often in the Italian climate; thin, sickly, wrinkled,

with a long bird's beak topped by a pair of glasses, a bony hand, a sardonic mouth, he floats in his baggy clothes]; P. de Musset, *En voiturin*, 992; de Maupassant, *La vie errante*, 246–47.

40. For the blatant chauvinism that marked certain French travelers, see Jules Dupré, "O France! beau pays de France. . . . Je parcours toutes les cités les plus renommées de l'Italie, je cherche vainement une ombre de ta grandeur, de ta magnificence" [Oh France! beautiful country. . . . I travel through all the most famous cities of Italy, I search in vain for a shadow of your greatness, of your magnificence]; *Relation d'un voyage en Italie*, 742; and Charles-Augustin de Sainte-Beuve, "Au retour de Paestum. En voyant dans ces lieux si beaux toute cette vermine, cette mendicité et cette bassesse qui est le fond, il me prend fréquemment de ces cris! O France libre et généreuse!" [Back from Paestum. Seeing in these beautiful places all that vermin, all that begging, all that depravity, as its background, I am overtaken frequently by the cry! Oh France! free and generous!]; *Voyage à Naples*, 744. In regard to the xenophobia directed against the English, see Chateaubriand, "multitude d'insipides anglaises et de frivoles dandys" [multitudes of insipid English women and frivolous dandys]; *Mémoires d'outre-tombe*, 1010; or Jules Janin, "L'Anglais est le mauvais génie de l'Italie" [The English are the evil demon of Italy]; *Voyage en Italie*, 1012.

41. "Paris, reine et capitale du monde, quelle ville peut l'être comparée?" [Paris, queen and capital of the world, what city can compare to you?]; Dupré, *Relation d'un voyage en Italie*, 742.

41. "Nous ne chargions pas non plus nos mains des redoutables volumes où l'on dit tout ce qu'il faut voir, et presque tout ce qu'il faut penser: prétention bien exhorbitante, malgré le mérite des auteurs" [We do not weigh ourselves down any more with those questionable volumes that tell us all we have to see, and almost all we ought to think: totally unreasonable pretention, despite the merit of the authors]; L. Veuillot, *Rome et Lorette*, 764. For the flattering clichés of tourist guidebooks, see M. A. Fusco, "Il luogo comune paesaggistico nelle immagini di massa," in *Storia d'Italia. Annali* 5 (1982): 753–802.

43. Stendhal, *Rome, Naples et Florence*, 157.

44. P. Bourget, *Sensations d'Italie*, 766–67.

45. See G. Ricci, "Gli incunabuli del Baedeker," *Ricerche storiche* 7 (1977); and L. Di Mauro, "L'Italia e le guide turistiche dall'Unità a oggi," *Storia d'Italia. Annali* 5 (1982): 369–430.

*Chapter 6: The Significance of
the Journey in Manzoni*

1. *Poesie e tragedie,* critical text by Fausto Ghisalberti, vol. 1 of *Tutte le opere di Alessandro Manzoni,* ed. Alberto Chiari and Fausto Ghisalberti (Milan: Mondadori, 1957).
2. *Opere morali e filosofiche,* ed. Fausto Ghisalberti, vol. 3 of *Tutte le opere* (Milan: Mondadori, 1962). I include the *Aggiunte e abbozzi.*
3. *Lettre à M. Chauvet sur l'unité de temps et de lieu dans la tragédie,* in Alessandro Manzoni, *Opere,* ed. Guido Bezzola, vol. 3 of *Opere varie* (Milan: Rizzoli, 1961).
4. *I Promessi Sposi,* rev. ed. of 1840, vol. 2, tome 1, *Tutte le opere* (Milan: Mondadori, 3d ed., 1963).
5. Other critics have considered various aspects of the journey in Manzoni; e.g. Gina Alani, *La struttura dei Promessi Sposi* (Berne: A. Francke, 1948), 23–39; Cesare Federico Goffis, "Da Porta Nuova a Porta Orientale: una traversata di redenzione," in *Studi sulla cultura lombarda in memoria di Mario Apollonio* (Milan: Vita e Pensiero, 1972), 1:388–403; Ezio Raimondi, "La ricerca incompiuta," in *Il romanzo senza idillio. Saggio sui promessi sposi* (Turin: Einaudi, 1974), 173–89; Giorgio Bárberi Squarotti, "Partenza e fuga: da Renzo e Lucia ad Anguilla," *Lettere Italiane* 28, no. 2 (1976): 160–77; Sandro De Feo, "Il diacono Martino e il viandante di Manzoni," in Giancarlo Vigorelli, *Manzoni pro e contro* (Milan: Istituto Propaganda Libraria, 1976), Novecento II, 22–37 (the original is from 1960); Franco Ferrucci, "Dal giardino di Candido alla vigna di Renzo," in Vigorelli, *Manzoni,* 399–409, esp. 403; Mary Ambrose, "Manzoni e Scott: il tempo nella struttura del romanzo," in *Atti del XI Congresso Nazionale di Studi Manzoniani,* Lecco, from 29 September to 3 October 1976 (Lecco: 1982), 363–76, esp. 367. I have not dealt with the author's journey through the material, accompanied naturally by the reader, since my interest is in Manzoni's view of life. A recent examination of this aspect is found in Elizabeth Meier-Brügger, *Fermo e Lucia e I promessi sposi come situazioni comunicative* (Frankfurt am Main: Peter Lang, 1987), 34–40.

Chapter 7: Verga, or The Impossible Journey

1. This paper contains numerous references—both direct and indirect—to the theoretical positions of M. Bakhtin and in particular to

the work *Voprosy literatury i estetiki*, Izdatel'stvo, "Chudozestvennaja literatura" (Moscow, 1975); cf. M. Bakhtin, *The Dialogic Imagination*, ed. Michael Holquist, trans. Caryl Emerson and Michael Holquist (Austin: University of Texas Press, 1981). For the analysis of the landscape in chapter 4, part 2 of *Mastro*, we refer to Northrup Frye, *Anatomy of Criticism: Four Essays* (Princeton: Princeton University Press, 1957). For the numerous references to W. Benjamin, see in particular *Upsprung des deutschen Trauerspiels* (Frankfurt am Main: Suhrkamp Verlag, 1963), translated into English as *The Origin of German Tragic Drama*, trans. J. Osborne (London: New Left Books, 1977), and *Das Passagen-Werk* (Frankfurt am Main: Suhrkamp Verlag, 1982). All page references to Verga's works are taken from Giovanni Verga, *Opere*, ed. Gino Tellini (Milan: Mursia, 1988).

2. Cf. Verga's letter to Capuana, 14 March 1879, in G. Verga, *Lettere a Luigi Capuana*, ed. G. Raya (Florence: Le Monnier, 1975), 112–15. In this letter Verga compares the notion of space-time of the countryside to that of big cities, which are marked by "turbulent and incessant passions" (114).

3. For a detailed analysis of this political thesis, see my "Sulla costruzione dei *Malavoglia*. Nuove ipotesi di lavoro," in *Verga. L'ideologia, le strutture narrative, il "caso" critico*, ed. R. Luperini (Lecce: Milella, 1982), 61–114.

4. According to L. Goldmann, *Pour une sociologie du roman* (Paris: Gallimard, 1964), 33, the novel of the twentieth century, from Kafka to Robbe-Grillet, is apparently characterized by "l'effort pour écrire le roman de la non-existence de toute recherche qui progresse" [the effort to write the novel about the nonexistence of any investigation leading to purposefulness]. In a note he adds, "Lukacs caractérisait le temps du roman traditionnel par la propostion: 'Le chemin est commencé, le voyage est terminé.' On pourrait caractériser le nouveau roman par la suppression de la première moitié de cet énoncé. Son temps serait caractérisé soit par l'énoncé: 'L'aspiration est là mais le voyage est fini' (Kafka, Nathalie Sarraute), soit simplement par la constatation que 'le voyage est déjà fini, sans que le chemin soit jamais commencé' (les trois premiers romans de Robbe-Grillet)" [Lukacs characterized time in the traditional novel by the proposition: 'The path is begun, the journey is finished.' One could characterize the nouveau roman by the suppression of the first half of that statement. Its time would be characteized either by the statement: 'The aspiration is there but the

journey is finished' (Kafka, Nathalie Sarraute), or simply by the statement that 'The journey is already over, without it ever having been started' (the first three novels by Robbe-Grillet)]. In Verga the journey is still possible, but only as a forced itinerary, which plunges into nothingness; it is devoid of meaning and is different from a search capable of arriving at a meaning and discovery. In short, *Mastro* is an integral part of the tradition of the bourgeois novel; however, by questioning its legitimacy, it contributes to its demise.

Chapter 8: The Journey in Ippolito Nievo's Narrative

1. G. Macchia, *Leopardi e il viaggiatore immobile*, in *Saggi italiani* (Milan: Mondadori, 1983), 258.
2. This aspect of Nievo's personality has been analyzed by P. V. Mengaldo in *L'epistolario di Nievo: una analisi linguistica* (Bologna: il Mulino, 1987).
3. In modern literary criticism this can be treated as a theme. Cf. C. Segre, *Avviamento all'analisi del testo letterario* (Turin: Einaudi, 1985), 331–59.
4. Ippolito Nievo, "La nostra famiglia di campagna," in *Novelliere campagnuolo e altri racconti*, ed. I. De Luca (Turin: Einaudi, 1956), 5–6.
5. Ibid., 3.
6. Ibid., 7.
7. Ibid., 6.
8. Ibid., 10, 19, 20. For the motif of the peasant who embodies a past "volto a diverso avvenire" [headed to a different future], see paragraph 14 of "La nostra famiglia di campagna."
9. This concept is even more evident in the second meeting between the travelers and Basilio, a peasant who is paradoxically happy with his destructive financial ignorance.
10. See, for example, the beginning of "Santa di Arra," in *Novelliere*, 62; or the first page of "Varmo," in *Novelliere*, 157–58.
11. Nievo, "Santa di Arra," 79.
12. The appeal exerted by urban customs upon the peasantry constitutes the narrative thread of the Mantua episode.
13. Nievo, "Varmo," 157–58.
14. S. Romagnoli, "Narratori e prosatori del Romanticismo," in *Storia della letteratura italiana* (Milan: Garzanti, 1968), 8:112.

15. Ippolito Nievo, *Le confessioni d'un Italiano* (Milan: Mondadori, 1981), 3–4, 53, 1070.

16. In this regard Mengaldo speaks of a "pulsione oggettivante che è anche fuga da sé" [the drive toward external objects that is also a flight from the self]. See his "Appunti di lettura sulle *Confessioni* di Nievo," in *Rivista di Letteratura Italiana* 3 (1984): 499.

17. See M. A. Cortini, *L'autore, il narratore, l'eroe* (Rome: Bulzoni, 1983), esp. chapter 3.

18. Or a short story without a "structure," as Carlino himself states. Critics—after having rejected the traditional interpretation, which on the one hand criticized and on the other approved the lack of narrative design in the novel—today have advanced three possible levels of interpretation emphasizing the three different stages of Carlino's life, without diminishing its integral qualities.

19. Nievo, *Le confessioni*, 1070. The lack of "structured order" is consciously manipulated by the narrator, demonstrated by the often repeated metanarrative characteristic of the transition from one stage to the next, of the change in rhythm and outline.

20. Ibid., 139.

21. Ibid., 509, 514, 519, 863, 867.

22. Ibid., 953; see also 1070.

23. See the month of cowardly contentment, as experienced by Carlino and the Pisana during the humiliation of the homeland. See also the episode of the growth of Carlino's wealth and status when he is an administrator during the Napoleonic rule of Bologna, a growth that parallels a significant vilification of his ideals, and also the figure of his morally bankrupt father.

24. "Il tempo non è tempo per chi ha danari a frutto: esso per me non fu mai altro che memoria, desiderio, amore, speranza" [Time is not time for someone who has money invested: for me it was never other than memory, desire, love, hope]; Nievo, *Le confessioni*, 535.

25. Ibid., 137–38, 357–58.

26. Mengaldo, "Appunti," 507.

27. Cf. "Il viaggio pedestre fino a Fratta, il riveder la Pisana . . . mi diedero troppo da pensare, da fare, da meditare" [The journey on foot as far as Fratta, and seeing the Pisana again, gave me too much to think about, to do, to meditate upon]; Nievo, *Le confessioni*, 357. "Rifaceva passo passo le corse di una volta; andava fino al Bastione di Attila . . . riandava alle memorie della mia infanzia, pensando quanto era fatto

diverso" [I retraced, step by step, the walks I used to take; I went as far as Bastione di Attila. . . . I went back to childhood memories, thinking about how different I was]; ibid., 367. "Ebbi il coraggio di offrire il braccio al Conte e alla Pisana . . . e di accomodarmi poi a cassetta col pretesto del caldo. . . . Mi ricordò allora alcuni anni prima quando . . . avea fatto quella strada stessa appeso alle coregge posteriori della carrozza. . . . Quanto insuperbii di vedermi mutato a quel segno!" [I had the courage to offer my arm to the Count and to the Pisana . . . and then to make myself comfortable on the coach-box with the pretext of the heat. . . . I was reminded then of some years before when . . . I had traveled the same road hanging on the straps behind the carriage. . . . How proud I was to see how much I had changed!]; ibid., 395. "Mano a mano che mi allontanava da quelle lagune per entrare in quel labirinto di fiumane, di scoli e di canali che uniscono a Venezia il basso Friuli, mi si abbuiavano nella mente le vicende di quell'ultimo anno, e quelli vissuti prima vi ricomparivano col guizzante barbaglio dei sogni. Mi pareva che la barca nella quale era mi rimenasse verso il passato" [Bit by bit as I moved away from those lagoons to enter into that labyrinth of swollen rivers, ditches, and canals that joins Venice to the lower Friuli, the events of the past year grew dimmer in my mind, and all the years lived previously before reappeared with the quivering dazzle of dreams. It seemed that the boat I was in was taking me back again toward the past]; ibid., 421–22. "Mentre la Pisana buona e spensierata faceva festa allo zio . . . io uscii pian piano a roppiccar conoscenza colle vecchie camere del Castello. . . . Mi ricordai" [while the good and lighthearted Pisana was welcoming the uncle, I sneaked out to reacquaint myself with the old rooms of the castle. I remembered]; ibid., 849.

28. Romagnoli wrote: "il vecchio Carlo presume di essere arrivato a una riva sicura . . . e non s'accorge di non aver chiuso i conti con se stesso, di essere, cioè, ancora, pur nella protratta vecchiezza in debito . . . con i propri sentimenti; a mano a mano che ricorda egli vi riaffonda dentro, li risuscita, ne riaccende la fiamma lontana ma ancora tutta bruciante, riapre ferite rimarginate" [Old man Carlo thinks he has reached a safe shore . . . and does not realize he has not settled accounts with himself, that is, he is still, even in his prolonged old age, in debt . . . to his own feelings: bit by bit as he remembers, he sinks back down into them, revives them, rekindles their distant but still burning flame, reopens healed wounds]; see his "Ippolito Nievo," in *Storia della cult-*

ura veneta. Dall'età napoleonica alla prima guerra mondiale (Vicenza: Neri Pozza, 1986), 6:184–85.

Chapter 9: Travel as Inspiration in Pascoli's Poetry

1. Homer, *Odyssey* 1.3.
2. Dante, *Purgatory* 8.3. Byron translates (*Don Juan* 3.108): "Soft hour! which wakes the wishes and melts the heart / of those who sail the seas on the first day / when they from their sweet friends are torn apart."
3. Percy Bysshe Shelley, "To a Skylark," v. 87.
4. "L'isola dei poeti," in Giovanni Pascoli, *Poesie*, with a note by Antonio Baldini (Milan: Mondadori, 1965), 735–37.
5. Pascoli, "Pietole," *Poesie*, 477–78.
6. Virgil, *Eclogue* 1.3.
7. Aristotle, *Metaphysics* 980.a.22, Cicero, *De finibus* 5.48.
8. Dante, *Inferno* 26.118–20.
9. Homer, *Odyssey* 13.190, 250: *géthesen dè polýtlas dîos Odysseús*.
10. The term *contaminatio* is understood in classical philology to be the imitation of more than one Greek model, as in a Roman comedy.
11. Pascoli, "Il ritorno," *Poesie*, 894.
12. Homer, *Odyssey* 11.121.
13. Ibid., 11.134. Cf. the Loeb edition of the *Odyssey* l.c. note.
14. Ovid, *Metamorphoses* 14.435–38.
15. Pascoli, "Il ritorno," *Poesie*, 895. Homer, *Odyssey* 5.135.
16. Pascoli, "L'ultimo viaggio (24 'Calypso')," *Poesie*, 996. A fine German translation of this poem with an illuminating introduction has been recently published by W. Hirdt (Tübingen: Narr, 1989). Cf. also E. Piras-Ruegg, *Giovanni Pascoli. L'ultimo viaggio. Introduzione, testo e commento*, Kölner Romanistische Arbeiten, no. 43 (Geneva: Droz, 1974).
17. "Jaufré Rudel," in Giosué Carducci, *Rime e ritmi* (Bologna: Zanichelli, 1939), 994.
18. Pascoli, "La mia sera," *Poesie*, 620.

Chapter 10: New and Traditional Forms of Nineteenth-Century Travel Literature

1. See, for example, P. Amat di San Filippo, *Biografia dei viaggiatori italiani colla bibliografia delle loro opere*, in *Studi biografici e biblio-*

NOTES TO PAGES 154–162

grafici sulla storia della geografia in Italia pubblicati in occasione del III Convegno Geografico Internazionale, 2d ed. (Rome: Società Geografica Italiana, 1882); A. D'Ancona, *Saggio di una bibliografia ragionata dei viaggi e delle descrizioni e dei costumi in lingue straniere* (1889; rpt. Ravenna: Tonini, 1970). And see also E. Bonora, "Presentazione," in A. D'Ancona, *Viaggiatori e avventurieri* (Florence: Sansoni, 1974), 13; G. Sgrilli, *Viaggi viaggiatori nella seconda metà del Settecento*, in *Miscellanea di studi critici pubblicati in onore di Guido Mazzoni dai suoi discepoli* (Florence: Tip. Galileiana, 1907), 1:277–308.

2. It is worth noting that Giovanni Battista Belzoni and Ippolito Rosellini were two of the principal exponents of a growing number of Egyptologists in Italy.

3. See note 1.

4. See G. Acerbi, "Lettere sull'Egitto," in *Biblioteca Italiana* 52 (1828): 3–13; 56 (1829): 137–61; 58 (1830): 282–85; 59 (1830): 145–64, 289–311. On Giuseppe Acerbi, see D. Visconti, *G.A.*, in *Dizionario biografico degli Italiani* (Rome, 1960), 1:134–36.

5. G. Acerbi, *Travels through Sweden, Finland and Lappland to the North Cape, in the Years 1798 and 1799*, 2 vols. (London: Mawman, 1802); *Voyage au Cap-Nord par la Suède, la Finland et la Laponie* (*traduction d'après l'original anglais revue sous les yeux de l'auteur, par J. Lavallée*), 3 vols. (Paris: Chez Levrault Sehoell et Comp. Libraires, 1804).

6. G. Acerbi, *Voyage au Cap-Nord*, 292–93.

7. G. Acerbi, in *Biblioteca Italiana* 59 (1830). See note 4.

8. See G. Rajberti, *Il viaggio di un ignorante*, ed. E. Ghidetti (Naples: Guida, 1985), 25.

9. Ibid., 27.

10. Ibid., 31.

11. See M. Dillon Wanke, "Introduzione," in G. Faldella, *A Vienna. Gita con il lapis* (Genoa: Costa and Nolan, 1983), 17.

12. Ibid., 246.

13. "L'itinerario faldelliano rivela un progressivo abbassamento della 'verve' inventiva e della mescidanza verbale che dall'ininterrotto impiego di accostamenti tra i piú eterogenei in *A Vienna* procede verso le intermittenze espressionistiche di *Viaggio a Roma* e perviene al codice piú normativo e regolarizzato di *A. Parigi*"; L. Surdich, "Introduzione," in G. Faldella, *A Parigi. Viaggio di Geronimo e Comp.* (Genoa: Costa and Nolan, 1983), 21–22.

14. Ibid., 232–33.

15. "L'anticonformismo del linguaggio non era in lui sostenuto da alcuna intenzione polemica, che ne volesse fare il segno di una rivolta anche morale e politica. Giustamente è stato scritto che la sua 'scapigliatura' si può in fondo riportare a una misura goliardica"; G. Ragazzini, "Introduzione," in G. Faldella, *L'Europa in provincia. Pagina di viaggio e di costume* (Milan: Longanesi, 1976).

16. "Fra pochi anni, io spero la letteratura fanciullesca sarà l'ultimo e più ridicolo portato della imbecille scurrilità e della menna stupidaggine italiana del periodo della liberazione: il capitano De Amicis parrà, salvo la dottrina e gli studi, il padre Aurelio Bertola"; G. Carducci, *Lettere*, Edizione Nazionale (Bologna: Zanichelli, 1942), 9:69, quoted by M. Dillon Wanke, "Introduzione," *A Vienna*, 25.

17. "[Molte pagine] sono miniate, disegnate, scolpite, tornite, finite, come io vorrei che fosse sempre la imaginosa e giovenil prosa italiana"; ibid.

18. G. Faldella, *A Vienna*, 134.

19. Ibid., 133.

20. See R. Frattarolo, "Edmondo De Amicis," in *Orientamenti culturali. Letteratura italiana: I minori* (Milan: Marzorati, 1962), 4:3107–10 ("La fortuna"). About the ideological meaning of De Amicis's "sentimentalism," see A. Asor Rosa, "La cultura" in *Storia d'Italia*, vol. 4: *Dall'Unità a oggi* (Turin: Einaudi, 1975), 2:932–33.

21. See G. Bertone, "La patria in piroscafo. Il viaggio di Edmondo De Amicis," introduction to *Sull'Oceano* (Genoa-Ivrea: Herodote, 1983), 12, 55.

22. "Nel momento in cui i cavalli vengono messi in pensione dall'elettricità e proprio nell'anno che inaugurava, insieme con la nascita d'una fabbrica d'automobili . . . un'era di produzione di altre tecnologie propulsive, nuovi trasporti e nuovi pendolarismi, urbani ed extra"; ibid., 51.

23. Italo Calvino, quoted by A. Ghirelli in his introduction to Renato Fucini, *Napoli a occhio nudo* (Turin: Einaudi, 1976), 9.

24. See F. Martini, "A Piedigrotta," in *Pagine raccolte* (Florence: Sansoni, 1912), 571–75.

25. "O montagne dalle nevi perpetue, a voi viene il fisico a studiare i fenomeni della temperatura e della luce; a voi il geologo bramoso di penetrare i misteri dei successivi rivolgimenti del globo; chiamate a voi, o montagne dalle perpetue nevi, un poeta, imponetegli nel vostro linguaggio sublime di ridire i vostri incanti e la vostra austera ed ami-

chevole maestà: spieghi egli a' volgari come fatica, per quanto grave, sia dolce a chi giunge a mirarvi da vicino, a baciare le vostre cime, ad afferrare le vostre roccie, a stringerle quasi in un amplesso affettuoso. Terribili e buone, voi infondete nei corpi il vigore e l'indulgenza negli animi" [Oh mountains with your perpetual snows, to you comes the physicist to study the phenomena of temperature and light; to you comes the geologist, eager to penetrate the mysteries of successive upheavals of the earth; call to you, oh mountains of perpetual snows, a poet, use your sublime language to force him to recount your enchantments and your austere friendly majesty, that he can explain to the common people how sweet the hardship is, no matter how exhausting, for those who succeed in coming close enough to admire you, to kiss your summits, and to cling onto your rocks, to enfold them almost in a passionate embrace. Terrible and great, you instill vigor in the body and endulgence in the soul]; F. Martini, "Su le Alpi," *Pagine raccolte*, 585.

Contributors

MEYER H. ABRAMS is professor emeritus of English at Cornell University.

CHRISTIAN BEC is professor of Italian at the University of Paris (Sorbonne). He is also vice-president of Associazione Internazionale per gli Studi di Lingua e Letteratura Italiana.

S. BERNARD CHANDLER is professor emeritus of Italian at the University of Toronto.

MARINELLA COLUMMI CAMERINO is professor of Italian at the University of Venice.

ELEANOR COOK is professor of English at Victoria University (University of Toronto).

GUSTAVO COSTA is professor of Italian at the University of California, Berkeley.

V. R. GIUSTINIANI is professor emeritus of romance philology at Albert Ludwig University, Freiburg.

ELVIO GUAGNINI is professor of Italian at the University of Trieste and chair of Dipartimento d'Italianistica.

ROMANO LUPERINI is professor of Italian at the University of Siena and chair of Dipartimento di Filologia e Critica della Letteratura.

ANTONINO MUSUMECI is professor of Italian at the University of Illinois, Urbana-Champaign.

G. SINGH is professor of Italian at Queen's University, Belfast.

Index

Abraham, 1, 2
Abrams, M. H., ix, 51
Acerbi, Giuseppe, 155–57
Aci Trezza, 80, 108–11, 122
Adam, 1, 71, 74, 81
Adda, 101
Addison, Joseph, 28
Aeneas, 71
Aetolus, 27
Africa, 88, 154
Albany, 46
Albion, 11
Alcman, 27
Alfieri, Vittorio, vii, 30–32
Allegory, 2, 6, 8, 44, 47, 71, 119
Allen, John, 31
Alps, ix, 144
Amat di San Filippo, 151, 154
Anacreon, 33
André, Marie, 22
Appennines, 90
Archetype, 47
Arctic, 154
Arethusa, 146
Aristotle, 29, 145
Arnold, Matthew, 61–62, 69
Asia, 11, 67, 154
Athena, 146
Atlantic Ocean, 164

Babylon, 33
Baedeker, Karl, 93
Bakhtin, M., 108, 124, 136
Barrès, Maurice, 84
Baudelaire, 60
Beauty, 40, 57
Bellay, Joachim du, 85
Benjamin, René, 119
Bertone, Giorgio, 165
Bible, 1–3, 6, 49
Bicocca, 109–10

Biella, 83
Bildungsroman, 114, 136, 139
Binni, Walter, 22
Blake, William, 11, 59
Bologna, 142
Bourget, Paul-Charles-Joseph, 85, 92
Brescia, 88, 133
Bresciani, Father, 161
Brofferio, Angelo, 161
Brosses, Charles de, 85, 89–90
Brown, H. F., 66
Browning, Robert, viii, 41ff., 66
Buddha, 66
Buenos Aires, 164
Bunyan, John, 8
Burke, Edmund, 22
Byron, George Gordon, 9, 26, 85, 89

Cain, 1, 9
Cairo, 155
Calvino, Italo, 165
Calypso, 6, 147–48
Camemi, 115–17, 119
Canziria, 115–16, 120, 122
Carducci, Giosuè, 142, 148, 162–63, 165
Carlyle, Thomas, 11
Catullus, 127, 130
Cervantes, Miguel de, 31
Cesarotti, Melchiorre, 22
Champollion, Jacques-Joseph, 155
Chateaubriand, François-Augustus-René de, 84–85, 89–90
Chaucer, Geoffrey, 56
Chauvet, M., 99
Christ, 2, 7, 95
Chronotope, 107, 111, 115, 121
Cicero, 29, 145
Circe, 6

Coleridge, Samuel, 9, 26, 57, 59
Colet, Louise, 90
Collegno, 83
Collodi, Carlo, 79
Columbus, 71
Comedy, 28–29
Comic, 21, 25–26, 28
Comines, Philippe de, 89
Correggio, 25
Crimea, 159
Criticism, feminist, 51

Daedalus, 71
D'Annunzio, Gabriele, 142
Dante, vii, 17, 20, 39, 44, 56, 61, 71, 89, 142, 145, 147, 149
da Verona, Guido, 80
De Amicis, Edmondo, 79, 163, 165
Defoe, Daniel, 125
Demogorgon, 11
Demosthenes, 24
de Musset, A., 90
de Musset, P., 91
Dickens, Charles, 165
Dillon, Matilde, 160
Donne, John, 56
Dumas, fils, Alexandre, 91
Duval, 161–62

Eden, 1–3, 8, 15, 74
Egypt, 1, 14, 154
Eliot, George, viii, 41 ff.
Eliot, T. S., 19, 20, 56
England, 8, 21, 26–29, 33–35, 40–41, 46, 56
Enlightenment, 10, 73
Edwardes, Charles, 66
Epic, 107, 112
Euripides, 27
Europe, 21–22, 29, 33, 37–38, 46, 73, 93, 95, 136, 154, 160
Eve, 1

Faldella, Giovanni, 160–62
Far East, 154
Ferrucci, Franco, 79

Fichte, Johann Gottlieb, 12–13
Fielding, Henry, 28
Finland, 156
Fiumegrande, 115–16, 122
Florence, 42, 46, 48–49, 90
Foscolo, Ugo, viii, 21ff., 75
Foucault, Michel, 82
France, 26–27, 29, 84–85, 91
Franchetti, Alberto, 122
Fratta, 136, 139
Friuli, 134
Frye, Northrop, 46
Fucini, Renato, 165

Garda, Lake, 127
Garibaldi, Giuseppe, 77
Gautier, Théophile, 85, 89–91
Germany, 8, 18, 26
Ghidetti, Enrico, 158
Giolio, 115–16
Giusti, Giuseppe, 70
Goethe, Johann Wolfgang von, 11, 22, 41, 85
Goupil, 161–62
Gozzi, Carlo, 89–90
Greece, 21–22, 26
Gritti, Francesco, 30

Hagar, 1
Hardy, Thomas, 60
Hegel, Georg Wilhelm Friedrich, 14–17
Heine, Heinrich, 161
Hölderlin, Friedrich, 11, 14
Hollander, John, 50
Holy Roman Empire, 52
Homer, vii, 6, 24, 39, 71, 75, 145, 147
Horace, 163
Houssaye, Arsène, 90
Humor, viii, 21–22, 26, 28–29, 31, 40, 161

Illusion, 53, 58, 66, 125
Imagination, 26, 54, 57–58, 126
Indies, 71

INDEX

Ionian Islands, 21
Irony, 29, 46, 57
Isaac, 1
Ishmael, 1
Isocrates, 29
Italy, viii, x, 21–22, 26, 35–36, 41–44, 46, 48–50, 52, 82, 84–85, 88, 90–91, 94, 99, 126–27, 141–42, 151, 155, 165
Ithaca, 147

Jacob, 1
James, 41ff.
Jason, 71
Jerusalem, 3, 7, 11
Jocasta, 27
Journey: bildungsreise, 12, 16, 41, 43, 46, 50–51; circuitous, 11, 13; circular, 2, 3, 7, 13, 15, 19; distance, 109; duration, 109; educational, viii, 10, 12–13, 17, 19, 43, 46, 51–52; emotional, 54; figurative, 17; Grand Tour, 17, 46, 52, 73, 85, 100, 141, 158; imaginary, 126; inner, 54; internal, 6; linear, 10; literal, 1, 14, 17; literary, 17, 50; metalepsis, viii, 41, 50, 139; metaphorical, 18; peregrinatio vitae, 1, 7–10, 12, 14, 17, 19, 20; philosophical, ix, 54; physical, 126, 134–35; psychological, 54; reading, 50; return, 107, 133; spiral, 10, 12; self-formative, 14–15; spiritual, 13, 18, 49, 52
Joyce, James, 145

Keats, John, 57
King Arthur, 8
Koran, 39

Lachaise, Père, 161–62
Lalonde, Joseph-Jérôme de, 85
Lamartine, Alphonse-Marie-Louis de Prat, 90
Lampredi, Urbano, 32

Lapland, 155–56
Leavis, F. R., 45
Legge Casati, 78
Leopardi, Giacomo, ix, 53ff., 75
Lessing, Gotthold Ephraim, 9–10
Lissa, Battle of, 81
Livingstone, David, 71
London, 100, 155
Longinus, 22, 24, 29–30, 39–40
Lydia, 27

Magellan, Ferdinand, 71
Mangalavite, 115
Mantua, 127, 144
Manzoni, Alessandro Francesco Tommaso Antonio, x, 74–75, 94ff., 149
Martini, Ferdinando, 165
Martino, Deacon of Ravenna, 97
Marx, Karl, 114
Massa, 142
Matera, 141
Maupassant, Guy, 84, 91
Mazzini, Giuseppe, 77
Meliboeus, 144
Memory, 28, 75, 97, 111–12, 121, 132, 139–40; recollection, 135, 139
Mendelssohn, Felix, 22
Mengs, Raphael, 22, 25
Merrill, James, 51
Messina, 142–43
Michelangelo, 25
Milan, 33, 100–101, 104, 158
Milton, John, 56, 62
Misson, Maxmilien, 85, 91
Mocenni Magiotti, Quirina, 34
Modernity, x, 26, 107, 112, 139
Montaigne, Michel, 85
Montesquieu, 85
Monticella, 161
Moses, 1, 2, 15, 71
Mount Etna, 143
Mount Pisgah, 1
Mount Sinai, 1, 15
Mount Snowden, 15

Mount Vesuvius, 90
Muir, Edwin, 60
Musset, 89

Naples, 90–91, 165
Napoleon, 27, 36, 95, 154
Nausicaa, 146
Neoplatonism, 6
New York, 46
Nievo, Ippolito, 18, 126ff.
North America, 46, 136, 141
North Cape, 155
Novalis, 11

Oceania, 154
Omar Khayyám, 69
Ovid, 75, 147

Padua, 90
Palermo, 115, 122
Pallas, Peter Simon, 40
Paris, 33, 91, 161
Parody, 127
Pascal, Blaise, 58, 70
Pascoli, Giovanni, x, 141ff.
Pasturo, 102
Pavese, Cesare, 81
Petrajo gorge, 116, 119
Petrarch, 89
Phidias, 24
Philoctetes, 31
Picaresque, 70
Piedigrotta, 165
Piedmont, 161
Pietole, 144
Pindemonte, 24, 127, 130
Pisa, 142
Pitt, Penelope, 30
Plotinus, 6, 13
Plutarch, 26–27
Po, 141
Polyneices, 27
Pope, Alexander, 29
Portogruaro, 136
Poseidon, 145–46
Pound, Ezra, 66

Proclus, 3, 6
Progress, 108, 110–11, 124
Prometheus, 11

Quinet, Edgar, 90
Quintilian, 29

Rabelais, François, 85
Ragazzini, Giorgio, 162
Raglan, Lord, 159
Rajberti, G., 158
Raphael, Raffaello, 25
Recanati, 75
Resegone, 101
Restoration, 36
Richter, Jean Paul, 26
Ricks, Christopher, 50
Risorgimento, 73, 77, 165
Rodari, G., 83
Romagna, 141
Roma, 33, 42, 45–46, 48–49, 52, 90
Rosellini, 155
Rousseau, vii, 135
Russell, Bertrand, 56

Saint Augustine, vii, 6
Saint Helena, 95
Saint John, 2
Saint Luke, 2
Saint-Non, 85
Saint Paul, 2
Salgari, 79
Sand, Georges, 90, 135
Schelling, Friedrich, 13
Schiller, Johann Christoph Friedrich von, 13
Scott, Sir Walter, 100
Scotti, Mario, 27
Sempion Pass, 90
Sesto Calende, 90
Shakespeare, vii, 45, 56, 62
Shelley, Percy Bysshe, 9, 11
Sicily, 143–44
Sirmione, 127
Socrates, 24
Solferino, 127

Sonnino, 122
Sonzogno, 160, 164
Sophocles, 31
South America, 164
Space, 107–8, 111, 150
Spain, 88
Sparta, 27
Spenser, Edmund, 8
Stanley, Sir Henry Morton, 163
Staël, Anne-Louise-Germaine de, 40
Stendhal, 84, 92
Sterne, Laurence, 21–22, 29, 158
Stockholm, 156
Sublime, viii, 21–22, 24–28, 40
Surdich, Luigi, 161
Sweden, 156
Swift, Jonathan, 71
Symbolism, 113, 120

Taine, Hyppolite, 90
Teiresias, 146
Theseus, 31
Time, 107–8, 111, 115, 120–21, 124
Topology, ix, 84
Torretta, 115

Tragedy, 28–29, 47, 96–97, 99
Treves, 160, 163
Truth, ix, 40, 53–61, 64–65
Turin, 83, 165
Turkey, 138
Typology, 50, 52, 84, 126, 134

Ulysses, 6, 21, 70–71, 142, 145–47
Una, 8

Venice, 22, 42, 48, 88–90, 136
Verga, Giovanni, x, 18–19, 80, 107ff.
Verne, Jules, 163
Versailles, 161–62
Vico, Giambattista, 25–26, 37, 54
Victoria Falls, 71
Vienna, 36, 160–61
Vienna, Congress of, 36
Virgil, 31, 71, 144
Vizzini, 115–16, 119, 122

Wordsworth, William, 14–15, 17–19, 56–59, 62, 65
Winckelmann, Johannes, 22
Wright brothers, 71

Zacynthos, 75